THE FABS

THE FABS

THE SCRAPBOOK OF A REVOLUTION

HANNAH HARSHE AND M. EARL SMITH

To the Fab 5, and to Michigan fans everywhere.
Give back our banners!

America Through Time is an imprint of Fonthill Media LLC
www.through-time.com
office@through-time.com

Published by Arcadia Publishing by arrangement with Fonthill Media LLC
For all general information, please contact Arcadia Publishing:
Telephone: 843-853-2070
Fax: 843-853-0044
E-mail: sales@arcadiapublishing.com
For customer service and orders:
Toll-Free 1-888-313-2665

www.arcadiapublishing.com

First published 2020

ISBN 978-1-63499-200-8

Typeset in Avenir
Printed and bound in England

CONTENTS

ACKNOWLEDGMENTS

The publishing process is a tiresome one. Between writing, researching, scanning, visiting archives, purchasing materials, communicating with co-authors, and the taxing nature of the material itself, we often find frustration past the point that the average human can bear. The folks at Fonthill Media—such as Alan Sutton, Jamie Hardwick, Matthew Rodriguez, and Kena Longabaugh—make this process considerably easier. Special thanks must also be given to coach Steve Fisher, who was willing to chat with us for a few minutes, as well as reviewing our manuscript.

For his part, Martin would like to thank his past co-authors: Jade Huguenin, Nayeli Riano, and Gus Ferres. He would also like to give a special thanks to Hannah, whose zeal and zest for this project made it what it is today. Special consideration must be given to Kate Sydnes, Nicole Flibbert, Henrique Laurino, Jasmine Raghunandan, Samantha Cooke, Caitlin Likens, Laura Williams McCaffrey, David Yoo, and Renee Watson. As always, Nick and Leah are the greatest children ever, and Che is the best Sheltie ever. I love you guys.

Hannah would like to thank her parents (and siblings) for raising her on Michigan basketball from day one and for always empowering her to tell stories. Special thanks to all the friends who have accompanied her to cheer on the maize and blue, whether that means taking a fifteen-minute ride on the Bursley-Baits bus or a twenty-four-hour car ride down to San Antonio. All the love in the world to Al, Iz, Lil, and Shan. Finally, a huge thank you to Martin for his tireless work and guidance on this project.

INTRODUCTION

I was born into a world that already belonged to the Fab 5. At the very moment when the University of Michigan doctors helped me breathe my first breath of crisp Ann Arbor air, Chris Webber was leading his team, the Washington Wizards, to a 110–87 victory against the Golden State Warriors. I was born in 1998, which was Webber's fifth season in the NBA and essentially the honeymoon phase of the Fab 5. The controversy that had accompanied the Fab 5's run at Michigan was finally a distant enough memory to merit rose-colored glasses. The stories of their relentless trash talk had become Michigan basketball lore. The long, baggy shorts had ceased to be a Fab 5 statement and had simply become normal basketball shorts. The banners were still hanging in Crisler, where one of my earliest memories involves sitting on my dad's lap eating popcorn and wearing a Jamal Crawford headband.

The world still belongs to the Fab 5 today, but their impact is just distant and controversial enough to make it a conversation starter. The banners came down from their home in Crisler when I was in kindergarten, and by the time I moved into my freshman dorm at Michigan, John Beilein had built a program that was nationally respected as one of the cleanest and classiest in the country. In many ways, I grew up in an era of Michigan basketball that was antithetical to the Fab 5 era.

During my sophomore year, I stared at the TV with my mouth hanging open as Michigan squeezed past Florida State to qualify for the 2018 Final Four. I had turned twenty a month prior, before the NCAA tournament bracket had even been released, and had told my parents to hold off on buying me any birthday presents; the only thing I wanted was a trip to San Antonio to watch Michigan play in the Final Four. As my birthday wish materialized before my eyes, I called my dad, who had driven to Minneapolis to cheer on Michigan's five freshmen in 1992. He passed down his stories about watching the Fab 5 the way other parents probably pass down family recipes.

My mom used to give me various Mitch Albom books to teach me how to write, and when one birthday I received a dog-eared copy of *The Fab Five*, I tore through it in under twenty-four hours. Whenever "the fans at Crisler" were mentioned, I could see myself cheering in the stands, squinting down at those five freshmen who were making basketball history. This kind of family lore is essentially what's keeping the Fab 5's legacy alive: copies of Mitch Albom's book passed on from mother to daughter, stories about the 1992 Final Four shared over the phone.

The Fab 5's wins may not be hanging from the rafters, but their legacy is woven into the seats and buried under the floorboards—not just at Crisler, but at every basketball arena in the country. The Fab 5 hand-crafted the sport of college basketball that we know and love today. Even if they had not won a single game (which, if you ask the record books, may in fact be the case), the lasting impact they had on the sport is undeniable and will remain in place for all time. As Jalen Rose puts it, UNC might have won the 1993 NCAA Championship, but do you remember the name of a single player off that roster?

Part of what makes the Fab 5's legacy difficult to appreciate today is that so much of what made them revolutionary has since become commonplace. Today, no one bats an eye when a college basketball player listens to rap music. Trash talking is a keystone of the game, and while today "one and done" players are critical to the perennial success of programs like Duke and Kentucky, the Fab 5 played at a time when seniors started and freshmen came off the bench, if they played at all.

While I thoroughly appreciate the lasting impact that the Fab 5 had on college basketball, I am particularly drawn to them because their legacy spills outside of Crisler and on to the streets of Ann Arbor, Ypsilanti, Detroit, and the world. They were and are more than just athletes, and it would be foolish to try to appreciate the Fab 5 without looking into the larger cultural narrative surrounding their experiences at Michigan. The Fab 5 boys were social activists: they were black and unapologetically influenced by urban culture, on a campus that is overwhelmingly white. Many of their most iconic and controversial moments on and off the court were, at their core, social movements, whether or not college basketball fans at the time had the cultural awareness to recognize that reality. Just look at the plain blue t-shirts, or the way Jalen Rose described his perception of the Duke rivalry, or, in certain instances, the blatant racism that Michigan fans directed toward their own team. If we speak about the Fab 5 without opening the door to conversations about race and social class, then we are ignoring perhaps the most important part of their legacy.

When M. Earl Smith reached out to me about co-authoring this book, we thought that we would be documenting history. The Fab 5 had played almost thirty years ago and had since "broken up." It was not until Michigan hired Juwan Howard as head coach, and Jalen Rose began speaking of the inevitability of a Fab 5 reunion, that we realized that we are still in the thick of the Fab 5 era. This book, then, is not so much documenting history as it is celebrating the five Michigan athletes who continue to revolutionize the sport of college basketball. It is a glance at the rafters where the banners once hung, and an acknowledgment of the work that is still to be done. After all, the world still very much belongs to the Fab 5. They never even lost possession.

Hannah Harshe
University of Michigan
Class of 2020

1
CHRIS WEBBER

A.K.A. MAYCE EDWARD CHRISTOPHER WEBBER II

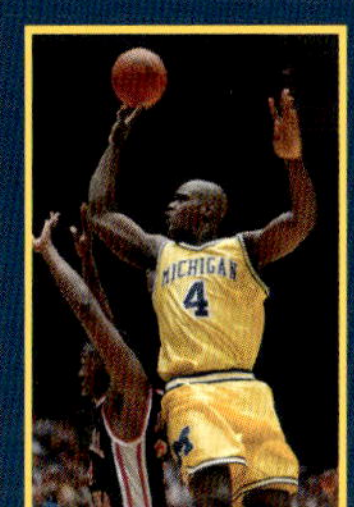

BORN: 1 March 1973, Detroit, Michigan

POSITION: Power forward/center

HEIGHT: 6 feet 10 inches

WEIGHT: 250 pounds

JERSEY NUMBER(S): 44 (HS); 4 (UM); 2, 4, 84 (NBA)

HIGH SCHOOL: Detroit Country Day School, Beverly Hills, MI

COLLEGE: University of Michigan (1991–1993)

NBA: Golden State Warriors (1993–1994, 2008); Washington Bullets/Wizards (1994–1998); Sacramento Kings (1998–2005); Philadelphia 76ers (2005–2007); Detroit Pistons (2007).

HIGH SCHOOL HONORS: Michigan's Mr. Basketball (1991); Naismith Prep Player of the Year (1991); Mr. Basketball USA (1991); McDonald's All-American Game MVP (1991); Dapper Dan All-Star Game MVP (1991); Three-time state champion (1989–1991)

COLLEGE HONORS: USBWA National Freshman of the Year (1992); Consensus first-team All-American (1993); finalist, John R. Wooden Award (1993, vacated); finalist, Naismith College Player of the Year (1993, vacated); Two-time NCAA Tournament Runner-up (1992, 1993, vacated).

PROFESSIONAL HONORS: NBA Rookie of the Year (1994); NBA Rebounding Leader (1999); Five-time NBA All-Star (1997, 2000–2003); All-NBA First Team (2001), Three-time All-NBA Second Team (1999, 2002, 2003); All-NBA Third Team (2000), #1 Overall pick in the 1993 NBA Draft; #4 retired by the Sacramento Kings.

CAREER AVERAGES (PER GAME)

LEVEL	POINTS	REBOUNDS	ASSISTS	STEALS	BLOCKS
College (2 yrs)	17.4	10.0	2.4	1.5	2.5
NBA (15 yrs)	20.7	9.8	4.2	1.4	1.4

Chris Webber was born on March 1, 1973, in Detroit, Michigan. Shown here in his high school years, Webber played high school basketball at Detroit's Country Day School, where he would start for four years, winning three MHSAA state championships. As a senior, Webber would average 29.4 points and thirteen rebounds per game. Webber's senior year would be filled with accolades, including being named "Michigan's Mr. Basketball," the National Player of the Year, and the MVP of both the McDonald's All-American and Dapper Dan All-Star games. Webber would commit to play college basketball at the University of Michigan.

Top right: This press photo shows Chris Webber before his freshman season at Michigan, as a member of the "Fab 5" recruiting class. As a freshman, Webber would average 15.5 points, ten rebounds, 2.2 assists, 1.6 steals, and 2.5 blocks, on 56 percent shooting. Webber would be named "National Freshman of the Year" by the United States Basketball Writers Association. A high point of Webber's season would be in the second round of the NCAA tournament, where Webber put up thirty points and nine rebounds against East Tennessee State University. (*Courtesy of the Bentley Historical Library, University of Michigan*)

Right: This is another press photo taken before Webber's freshman season at Michigan. Michigan would make a run, despite being no. 6 seed, to the national championship game, where they would fall to Duke by a score of 71–51. Webber would finish the national title game with fourteen points and eleven rebounds, recording a double-double that was nearly dead-on to his season averages of 15.5 points and ten rebounds, on 50 percent (six of twelve) shooting. For his post-season efforts, Webber would be named to the all-NCAA Tournament team. (*Courtesy of the Bentley Historical Library, University of Michigan*)

Shown here taking a long three-pointer, Chris Webber used his first home game at Crisler Arena against Chicago State on the campus of the University of Michigan as a coming-out party of sorts. Wearing the long, baggy shorts that would become a Fab 5 trademark (although in an era before pulled-up black socks would become part of the ensemble), Webber would lead the team with seventeen points on 8–10 shooting, although he would miss the three-pointer shown here. (*Courtesy of the Bentley Historical Library, University of Michigan*)

Michigan would go on to beat Chicago State by a final of 112–62, in the first home game for the Fab 5. Webber, shown here dunking, was an awesome offensive force, going eight for ten on his way to seventeen points, which was scored in twenty-seven minutes of court time. Webber was a force on the boards, gathering in two offensive and nine defensive rebounds, giving him eleven on the night, which, while one above his season average, would put him on pace for fifteen over a forty-minute game. (*Courtesy of the Bentley Historical Library, University of Michigan*)

Chicago State would fall victim to another awesome dunk by Chris Webber, unable to stop him from imposing his will at the basket. The ease in which Webber scored made other facets of his game obsolete, as Chicago State did not have the physical structure or the desire to stop Webber close to the rim. Webber took no foul shots for the game. His ability to score at ease precluded the need for him to facilitate to his other teammates, but still, he was credited with five assists. (*Courtesy of the Bentley Historical Library, University of Michigan*)

Although Webber's offensive prowess cannot be denied (as many of the action shots of him in the Bentley archives are of him dunking), Webber was a defensive force as well. Aside from rebounding, Webber was also an asset in the blocks department, putting up three against an undersized Chicago State team. So overpowering was the Fab 5's debut, in fact, that Webber, who averaged nearly two steals a game, had only one. (*Courtesy of the Bentley Historical Library, University of Michigan*)

HYDRA-
HOWARD
25
WEBBER
4
6:48

Previous page: Two games later, the young upstarts of the Fab 5 would take on top-ranked Duke in a game that would show that the young upstarts were the real deal. Despite being heavy underdogs, the young Wolverines would, on the strength of double-digit scoring by all five players, take the top-ranked Blue Devils to the brink, losing in overtime by a score of 88–85. Despite their youthful inexperience, the Fab 5 had taken the defending national champions to the edge, showing that they belonged on the court with anyone. (*Courtesy of the Bentley Historical Library, University of Michigan*)

Webber, and his Fab 5 cohorts, showed that they could play with the best teams in the nation. For his part, Webber had a stellar game, scoring twenty-seven points, twelve rebounds, three assists, four blocks, and a steal in thirty-nine minutes. His defensive skills were key in holding a Duke team in check that boasted the future top-seven NBA Draft picks in Bobby Hurley, Grant Hill, and Christian Laettner. In spite of the defeat, Michigan would become one of the few teams to move up in the rankings after a loss. (*Courtesy of the Bentley Historical Library, University of Michigan*)

The Fab 5 would rebound in their next game, against in-state opponent Central Michigan. The Wolverines would defeat the Chippewas by a score of 86–70. Webber, shown here with a fist raised in celebration, would have a remarkable game, scoring sixteen points (on 5–11 shooting and 5–8 from the charity stripe), twelve rebounds, two assists, and a thunderous six blocks—a career high. For the year, the Wolverines would score a 3–1 record against in-state opponents. (*Courtesy of the Bentley Historical Library, University of Michigan*)

Shown here, awaiting a pass, is Chris Webber, in action against Big Ten rival Northwestern on February 22, 1992. The Wolverines would knock off the Wildcats by a score of 76–63, which improved them to a 17–6 mark on the season, including an 8–5 mark in the Big Ten. For his part, Webber had a stellar game, scoring fourteen points (on seven of thirteen shooting), grabbing six rebounds, tallying three assists, grabbing two steals, and blocking three shots in a light twenty-four minutes of work. (*Courtesy of the Bentley Historical Library, University of Michigan*)

Shown left, in 1991, is Chris Webber, taking part in an exhibition between the University of Michigan Wolverines and the Cuban national team. Despite the embargo that was placed by President Kennedy, the two nations still interact when matters of cultural exchange are involved, including sports. For Webber's part, he was never a big part of the US national team's plans. His career in college started around the same time that professional players were invited to the Olympiad, and it was Duke rival Christen Lattenter that was chosen to be the college representative for the original "Dream Team." (*Courtesy of the Bentley Historical Library, University of Michigan*)

Although Webber did not play for the national team, he did spend some time, in odd situations, playing abroad. For example, after the 1991–1992 season, coach Steve Fisher took his young team on a trip to Europe, where they saw the sights and played several international teams. Overseas would cause some trouble for Webber, as, in 1998, he was fined for marijuana possession while doing promotional work for the Fila shoe company in Puerto Rico. Webber would later be awarded a $2.61-million settlement for breach of contract relating to the incident. (*Courtesy of the Bentley Historical Library, University of Michigan*)

This photo shows Chris Webber and Jalen Rose, Fab 5 cohorts, during a home game against Indiana on March 8, 2018. The game would be a great triumph for the young Wolverines, as they would knock off the second ranked team in the country, 68–60. This win avenged an 89–74 loss at Indiana on January 21. Webber would have a stellar game, scoring eleven points and grabbing a monstrous eighteen rebounds in thirty-two minutes of floor time. Rose would score fifteen points, with four rebounds and four assists, in a game where he led the Wolverines with thirty-six minutes of floor time. (*Courtesy of the Bentley Historical Library, University of Michigan*)

Six days later, Webber would lead the Wolverines to another Big Ten victory, this time over the Illinois Fighting Illini, by a tally of 68–59. The win would move the Wolverines to a 20–8 record, which included an 11–7 record in what was a tough Big Ten conference. This win gave the Wolverines a season sweep of Illinois, as they had beat them on the road on January 18 by a score of sixty-eight to sixty-one. Webber, for the game, scored thirteen points, pulled down four rebounds, and blocked a team-leading three shots. (*Courtesy of the Bentley Historical Library, University of Michigan*)

Above: Shown in a state of exhaustion, Chris Webber could not be blamed for being a little tired after his career at Michigan. In two seasons, Webber started each of Michigan's seventy games. Michigan would boast a record of 56–14 in those two seasons, with two runner-up appearances in the NCAA Tournament national championship game. In his freshman year, Webber averaged thirty-two minutes a game, and in his sophomore season, he averaged 31.8 minutes a game, for a career average of 31.9 minutes per game. With 1,088 in the former and 1,143 in the latter, Webber played 2,231 minutes (37.19 hours) of basketball in his time at Michigan.

Right: If the Fab 5 were known for anything, it was trash talk, especially among the likes of Juwan Howard, Jalen Rose, and Chris Webber. Yet while Howard and Rose used the former as part of their toolbox, for Webber, trash talk was personal. After some vitriol from the University of Cincinnati Bearcats, Webber went out and led the Wolverines with a sixteen-point, eleven-rebound performance. Trash talk was part of the way that the younger Webber oozed confidence, which was on full display with an exhibition against the Dream Team, where he refused to back down from Larry Bird, Charles Barkley (who he dunked on), and Patrick Ewing, among others.

Shown here, in his team photo before the 1992–1993 season, is Chris Webber. A sophomore, Webber would, along with his Fab 5 comrades, lead Michigan back to the national championship game. For the season, Webber averaged a double-double, with 19.1 points, 10.1 rebounds, 2.5 assists, 1.4 steals, 2.5 blocks, and an average of thirty-two minutes per game. In thirty-six games, Webber shot nearly 62 percent from the floor. Webber was named team MVP and led an effort that set a Big Ten record for shots blocked by a team (193), a record that would stand until 2000. (*Courtesy of the Bentley Historical Library, University of Michigan*)

Coach Steve Fisher loved to put his players in games against international talent, both in Europe and at home. Webber and his Fab 5 partners played several of these games, including a November 23, 1992, preseason tilt against a team known as Ragnone Attorney AAU. The team, consisting of amateurs, who were playing AAU ball as it was on the cusp of being integrated into mainstream recruiting, beat the Wolverines in overtime, 122–121. Some 7,200 people filed into Crisler Arena for what would amount to a glorified scrimmage, just four days after the Wolverines defeated the Russian National Team. (*Courtesy of the Bentley Historical Library, University of Michigan*)

In spite of the defeat, it was not all bad news for the Wolverines. Although slightly embarrassed by the loss, it had no bearing on their season, and it was a dunk-filled, crowd-pleasing tilt. Webber led the Wolverines efforts, scoring twenty-eight points in as many minutes, to go with three rebounds and three assists, on eleven of eighteen shooting. More importantly, Webber managed to avoid any form of injury from the scrimmage, and the young team was well-prepared for the obstacles that would face them in the upcoming season. (*Courtesy of the Bentley Historical Library, University of Michigan*)

Fresh off the heels of a 1–1 start, which saw the Wolverines defeat Rice on the road by a tally of 75–71 and lose to fourth ranked Duke by a tally of 78–69, the Wolverines returned home to play their first home tilt of the season, against unranked Detroit. The Wolverines would take the win against the Titans by a score of 92–77. Chris Webber, shown here, takes a three-point attempt in what would be a wildly successful game for Michigan. Even Webber was in rare form, as he topped his season average in both three-point percentage and in free throw percentage. (*Courtesy of the Bentley Historical Library, University of Michigan*)

The game versus Detroit would be a high point for Webber in many ways. The sophomore sensation would score twenty-four points, accounting for over a quarter of Michigan's points. This was done on ten of fourteen shooting, which include one of two shooting from the three-point stripe and three of five shooting from the charity stripe. He pulled down a monstrous fourteen rebounds (five offensive and nine defensive) and managed six assists, well above his career average. On the defensive end, he contributed three blocks and a steal to the Wolverine victory. (*Courtesy of the Bentley Historical Library, University of Michigan*)

Shown here before the Wolverine's January 26, 1993, tilt with fierce rival Ohio State, is Chris Webber, donning a protective mask due to a broken nose suffered in a team practice a week prior. Michigan had beaten Minnesota and Illinois shortly after the accident, so their 72–62 win over the Buckeyes, even with Webber's injury, was not a shock. Webber, for his efforts, tallied twenty points and fourteen rebounds in thirty-four minutes of action. This included a seven of twelve shooting effort, three assists, two steals, and two blocked shots. (*Courtesy of the Bentley Historical Library, University of Michigan*)

Webber and his Fab 5 teammates had lost, on January 31, to an eleventh-ranked Iowa team. On March 2, the Wolverines sought, and received, revenge, beating the Hawkeyes by a tally of 82–73, at Crisler Arena. This improved their overall record to 23–4. In twenty-four minutes, Webber was not much of a factor, only contributing six points on a pale two of eight shooting effort. He did manage to make three steals, but Webber, in a rare move for him, fouled out well before the game was decided. It was one of just nine times that Webber would foul out of a contest. (*Courtesy of the Bentley Historical Library, University of Michigan*)

Next page, above: Five days later, bitter in-state rivals Michigan State would make their way to Crisler Arena. The Fab 5 was 2–1 against their in-state rivals, and this game represented their chance to end the season with a two-game lead. In the last game that the entire group would play against the Spartans, they emerged the victors by a score of 87–81, in overtime. Playing a robust thirty-seven minutes, Webber, who was in consideration for several postseason awards, recorded a double-double, with twenty-one points, fourteen rebounds, an assist, and two blocked shots. (*Courtesy of the Bentley Historical Library, University of Michigan*)

Next page, below: This photo shows Chris Webber and Coach Steve Fisher discussing strategy against Iowa. For the pair's time together, they would post a 3–1 record against the Hawkeyes. On January 9, 1992, Michigan went to Iowa and won by a score of 80–77. On February 12, 1992, the Wolverines beat Iowa at home by a score of 79–74. On January 31, 1993, Iowan, ranked eleventh, came into Michigan and beet the fifth-ranked Wolverines by a score of 88–80. Michigan, ranked fourth, would get their revenge on the then-fifteenth ranked Hawkeyes, taking the March 2, 1993, game, by a score of 82–73. (*Courtesy of the Bentley Historical Library, University of Michigan*)

Right: Michigan finished the regular season with a record of twenty-seven and four, with a Big Ten record of fifteen and three, which was good enough for a conference runner-up position behind rivals Indiana. Given the no. 1 seed in the West bracket of the 1992–1993 NCAA tournament, the Wolverines did not disappoint, routing sixteenth seed Coastal Carolina by a score of 84–53. Webber had a relaxed opening game. He tallied just twenty-four minutes in the matchup, scoring eleven points, grabbing seven rebounds, and tallying four assists, two steals, and two blocks. (*Courtesy of the Bentley Historical Library, University of Michigan*)

Below: The next round would prove tougher for the Wolverines, as they faced ninth-seeded UCLA, a national powerhouse with a long and storied tradition. There would be no early night for Webber, as the Wolverines would need all forty-two minutes of his effort to stop the Bruins from pulling the upset. In overtime, Michigan knocked off UCLA by a score of 86–84. Webber would score twenty-four key points, pull down a crucial fourteen rebounds, dish out two assists, record two steals, and block one shot, all while helping Michigan and the Fab 5 to the Sweet Sixteen.

Chris Webber and Jalen Rose had much to celebrate, as their efforts would take the Wolverines to their second straight Final Four. In the round of sixteen, Michigan would beat George Washington by a score of 72–64. Webber would score fourteen points, grab nine rebounds, and block two shots. In the Elite Eight, Michigan would beat Temple by a score of 77–72. Webber would score thirteen points, grab twelve rebounds, and block five shots. *(Courtesy of the Bentley Historical Library, University of Michigan)*

Third-ranked Michigan and second-ranked Kentucky would play one of the greatest Final Four games in the history of the NCAA Tournament on Saturday, April 3, 1993. Webber and teammate Rob Pelinka would have much to celebrate, as the Wolverines knocked off the Wildcats in overtime by a score of 81–78. In thirty-nine grueling minutes, Webber offered a stellar effort, putting up twenty-seven points and pulling down thirteen monstrous rebounds. On the defensive end, Webber managed to provide three crucial blocks.

As delightful as Webber's season had been, a crucial mistake in the National Championship game has become the career highlight of Webber's career at Michigan. With seconds left, and the Wolverines down by three, Webber advanced the ball up court, only to call a timeout when Michigan had none remaining. A technical foul was called, North Carolina was awarded two free throws and possession, and would go on to win the game by a score of 77–71. For the game, Webber would score twenty-three points and pull down eleven rebounds. He was named to the all-tournament team.

Shown here with on-court rival Grant Hill, Chris Webber signs autographs for a young fan sometime after the 1993 NCAA Tournament. Webber and Hill were fierce rivals on the court, with Hill's Duke Blue Devils posting a 3–0 record against Webber's Wolverines. In those games, Webber averaged 18.4 points, 12.4 rebounds, 3.4 assists, and 2.4 blocks per game. For his part, Hill would go on to an NBA career where he averaged 16.7 points, six rebounds, and 4.1 assists per game while playing for Detroit, Atlanta, Phoenix, and the Los Angeles Clippers. (*Courtesy of the Bentley Historical Library, University of Michigan*)

Shown here shortly before the 1993 John R. Wooden Award ceremony is, from left to right, Penny Hardaway, Coach John Wooden, and Chris Webber. Hardaway had an astounding career in his own right. In two seasons at Memphis State University, Hardaway averaged twenty points, 7.7 rebounds, and 5.9 assists per game. He did this while averaging a whopping 36.7 minutes per game. For his NBA career, Hardaway would, after being drafted no. 3 by the Golden State Warriors, average 15.2 points, 4.2 rebounds, and 5.5 assists per game. (*Courtesy of the Bentley Historical Library, University of Michigan*)

For his efforts on the court, Chris Webber was named the winner of the 1993 John R. Wooden Award, awarded to the nation's most outstanding player. In thirty-six games, Webber would average, in 31.8 minutes, 19.2 points, 10.1 rebounds, 2.5 assists, 1.4 steals, and 2.5 blocks per game. His Michigan team, led by him and his Fab 5 cohorts, would post a record of thirty-one wins and five losses, including a 15–3 record in Big Ten Play. He was also named the Naismith College Basketball Player of the Year and would go on to be the top pick, by the Orlando Magic, in the 1993 NBA Draft. He would be traded during the draft for Penny Hardaway, to the Golden State Warriors. (*Courtesy of the Bentley Historical Library, University of Michigan*)

As with any popular player, autograph culture plays a big part in the career of Chris Webber, shown here signing a program for a young fan at the John R. Wooden Award ceremony. Recently, there were ninety-seven available autographs available online of Webber to purchase, including certified trading cards, photographs, jerseys, ball caps, programs, basketballs, and index cards. Webber's popularity, which began during his Fab 5 days at Michigan, preservers to this day. (*Courtesy of the Bentley Historical Library, University of Michigan*)

Chris Webber, shown here signing an autograph before the John R. Wooden Award ceremony, has a complex relationship with the press. In his two seasons at Michigan, Webber would often struggle with postgame interviews, especially after a tough loss. There were also some tough moments after the Ed Martin scandal erupted. That being said, Webber has become a fine analyst himself, on NBA TV's *NBA Gametime Live*, as well as on TNT's *Inside the NBA*. He also hosts a podcast on Podcast One called *Fearless or Insane*. (*Courtesy of the Bentley Historical Library, University of Michigan*)

In a strange twist, Webber would only spend two seasons with the team that traded for him on draft night—his first and his last. As a rookie, Webber would play in seventy-six games for Golden State, averaging 17.5 points, 9.1 rebounds, 3.6 assists, 1.2 steals, 2.2 blocks, and 32.1 minutes per game. His efforts would see him named Rookie of the Year for the 1993–1994 season. His career would end in 2007–2008 with a nine-game stint for the Warriors, where he averaged 3.9 points, 3.8 rebounds, two assists, half a steal, and 0.7 blocks in an average of fourteen minutes played.

Shown here in the twilight of their careers are Chris Webber and Joe Smith. Webber and Smith had a lot in common. They both played in institutions that are now in the Big Ten (Michigan and Maryland). They were both primarily power forwards. They both started their careers in the NBA at Golden State. They were both the top overall pick in their draft class. They were both All-Americans who won national Naismith Player of the Year awards. They are even both 6 feet 10 inches.

Due to his role in the Ed Martin scandal, Chris Webber was forced to distance himself from the University of Michigan. With hurt feelings on both sides, reconciliation seemed unlikely. However, some thaws have taken place. Webber attended Michigan's win in the 2017 NCAA national championship game, viewing the title from a luxury box. Shown here in 2018, Webber would be on the field with the Wolverines football team as an honorary captain for the team's 2018 matchup against Penn state. Webber's return home, some say, is long overdue.

In spite of the circumstances surrounding his time at the University of Michigan, Webber (and his role in the Fab 5) remains a fond memory for both Michigan fans and basketball fans alike. Webber was the top recruit and the most decorated player in a recruiting class that led to a seismic shift in how the game of college basketball was both presented and perceived. In seventy games, Webber gave the University of Michigan every drop of effort that he could muster, and, in return, he was able to lead the program to heights that no one thought imaginable. He remains a decorated part of Michigan basketball lore.

2
JALEN ROSE

BORN: 30 January 1973, Detroit, Michigan

POSITION: Guard/small forward

HEIGHT: 6 feet 8 inches

WEIGHT: 210 pounds

JERSEY NUMBER(S): 42 (HS); 5 (UM); 5, 8 (NBA)

HIGH SCHOOL: Southwestern High School, Detroit, MI

COLLEGE: University of Michigan (1991–1994)

NBA: Denver Nuggets (1994–1996); Indiana Pacers (1996–2002); Chicago Bulls (2002–2004); Toronto Raptors (2004–2006); Phoenix Suns (2006–2007); New York Knicks (2007).

HIGH SCHOOL HONORS: Parade Second-Team All-American (1991); Detroit High School Hall of Fame (2013); Michigan Basketball Hall of Fame (2017); Two-time state champion (1990–1991)

COLLEGE HONORS: Consensus second-team All-American (1994); Two-time NCAA Tournament Runner-up (1992, 1993, vacated); Three-Time NCAA Tournament Elite Eight (1992–1994).

PROFESSIONAL HONORS: NBA All-Rookie Second Team (1995); NBA Most Improved Player (2000); no. 13 Overall pick in the 1994 NBA Draft; NBA Player of the Week (2000); Professional Basketball Writers Association Magic Johnson Award Honoree (2003); Naismith Memorial Basketball Hall of Fame Mannie Jackson Basketball's Human Spirit Award (2016).

CAREER AVERAGES (PER GAME)

LEVEL	POINTS	REBOUNDS	ASSISTS	STEALS	BLOCKS
College (3 yrs)	17.5	4.7	3.9	1.2	0.3
NBA (13 yrs)	14.3	3.5	3.8	0.8	0.3

Michigan basketball fans were familiar with Jalen Rose long before he suited up for his first game as a Wolverine. As one of the stars of the no. 2 ranked high school basketball team in the nation and a member of what many called "the greatest recruiting class of all time", fans expected a lot from Rose's freshman year at Michigan, and he delivered. Rose immediately secured a spot in the starting lineup and averaged 17.6 points per game his freshman year, earning an NCAA All-Tournament award. (*Courtesy of the Bentley Historical Library, University of Michigan*)

On Rose's first day in the gym with the team, the upperclassmen began dividing the players into teams for a scrimmage. True to nature, Rose insisted that instead of randomized teams, the five freshmen play the five best upperclassmen. Without a hint of remorse, the freshmen trash-talked their way to winning five of the five pickup games against the upperclassmen. After just one day in the gym, Rose had exposed the talent of the five freshmen, but, perhaps more importantly, he had established a stark, somewhat hostile, divide between the Fab 5 and the rest of the team. (*Courtesy of the Bentley Historical Library, University of Michigan*)

Rose's father, Jimmy Walker, was the first overall pick in the 1967 NBA draft and a two-time All-Star. When Rose was in sixth grade, Sam Washington, the director of the famous St. Cecilia's gym in Detroit, introduced Rose to Walker by showing him a highlight reel of Walker playing in the NBA. Rose never met his father, but he was inspired by his goal that someday his father would know his name. Today, Walker and Rose are the only father-son duo in NBA history in which each has scored over 10,000 NBA points. (*Courtesy of the Bentley Historical Library, University of Michigan*)

In the Wolverines' 84–63 exhibition win against the Cuban Nationals on November 14, 1991, Rose was not included in the starting lineup, but he made an impact off the bench, stepping into the role of point guard and ending the first half as the team's leading scorer. After the game, Coach Fisher praised Rose's passing ability and decision making. However, the Wolverines still had a long way to go; they had over thirty turnovers in this game and would later be criticized for their undisciplined playing style. (*Courtesy of the Bentley Historical Library, University of Michigan*)

Both on and off the court, Rose was known for his charismatic personality and bold self-confidence. His style was influenced by hip-hop culture, where baggy clothing was the norm. When the team first received their uniforms, Rose traded shorts with Chip Armer, who, at 6 feet 9 inches, wore the biggest size on the team. This trade began one of the Fab 5's greatest legacies—changing the popular fit of basketball shorts from short and tight to long and baggy. Pictured here next to a player from the Cuban national team, the difference in fit of shorts is easy to spot. (*Courtesy of the Bentley Historical Library, University of Michigan*)

The Wolverines started the 1991–1992 season on a four-game win streak against Detroit, Cleveland State, Chicago State, and Eastern Michigan (pictured here). Although the team was able to showcase its basketball I.Q. and athleticism throughout these four wins, the real test would come during their fifth game against the Duke Blue Devils, the reigning national champion. Michigan lost against Duke in overtime 85–88, but they "shocked the world" by keeping it close the whole game. (*Courtesy of the Bentley Historical Library, University of Michigan*)

In an era before one-and-dones, when playing time was typically determined by seniority, Coach Fisher began the season with three freshmen in his starting lineup: Jalen Rose, Chris Webber, and Juwan Howard. By February, Jimmy King and Ray Jackson would also be starting, meaning the starting lineup would consist only of all "Fab 5" freshmen. The young starting lineup garnered national attention, as well as dismay from upperclassmen who felt they had earned a starting position. (*Courtesy of the Bentley Historical Library, University of Michigan*)

Pictured here is Rose hitting a jump shot against in-state opponent Central Michigan University. Just two days prior, Michigan had caught the nation by surprise by putting up a close fight against no. 1 ranked Duke. Although the young Wolverines were not able to pull off an upset against the Blue Devils, they responded to the loss by entering a five-game win streak and securing double-digit wins against Central Michigan, Rice, and Virginia Tech. (*Courtesy of the Bentley Historical Library, University of Michigan*)

Pictured here is Rose during a December 21 game against Rice. Michigan beat Rice 87–70, and Rose was the team's leading scorer in this game, with a total of nineteen points, and the second leading rebounder with four rebounds. (*Courtesy of the Bentley Historical Library, University of Michigan*)

The Wolverines went 1–2 in their first three Big Ten games in January, including a home 60–65 loss to Purdue, pictured here. The key to Purdue's win was stopping Jalen Rose from driving. It worked; Purdue's defense forced Rose outside, and he did not have a field goal until the final minutes of the game, when he scored five consecutive points and cut the deficit to 56–53. Unfortunately for the Wolverines, that one-score deficit was the closest they came to beating the Boilermakers, but it showcased Rose's importance to Michigan's offensive output. (*Courtesy of the Bentley Historical Library, University of Michigan*)

Despite Michigan's talent and athleticism, the team's lack of discipline was an increasing liability, as made evident against Purdue, when the Wolverines were outrebounded 40–20. After the game, Purdue seniors Craig Riley and Woody Austin credited the win to their experience, contrasted with the youth of Michigan's starting lineup. Michigan's freshmen were criticized for being overly confident in the face of the senior-laden Boilermakers. This criticism should come as a surprise to no one; Michigan's freshmen, especially Jalen Rose, were known for their confidence and swagger, even in games when they perhaps should have been a bit more wary. (*Courtesy of the Bentley Historical Library, University of Michigan*)

By late February, the team had developed a cohesive identity, and Jalen Rose had grown comfortable as a leader. Pictured here is a game against Minnesota, in which Michigan won 95–70. Rose only put up ten points, which was low for him, but Coach Fisher praised the whole team for its defensive efforts. Earlier in the season, Minnesota had beaten Michigan by nine points. This game served as a testament to the team's development throughout the season. (*Courtesy of the Bentley Historical Library, University of Michigan*)

In early March, the Wolverines beat the second-ranked Indiana Hoosiers 68–60. Rose, who had been held to five points the last time they had played Indiana, was happy to exact his revenge upon the Hoosiers. "We may have spoiled (Indiana's) chances of possibly winning the Big Ten title outright," Rose said in a characteristically smug fashion. "But we don't mind playing the role of spoiler." After this victory, the Wolverines finally felt confident that they would secure a spot in the NCAA tournament. (*Courtesy of the Bentley Historical Library, University of Michigan*)

In Michigan's last game of the 1991–1992 regular
season, they beat Illinois 68–59 for their twentieth
win of the season. Rose led the team in scoring
with twenty-two points. Shortly after the game,
the team found out that they would go into the
NCAA tournament as no. 6 seed, which was a
lower seed than most had expected. Fortunately,
the seeding did not seem to hurt Michigan too
significantly, as the team won its way to the 1992
National Championship game, where it would
face the Duke Blue Devils. (*Courtesy of the
Bentley Historical Library, University of Michigan*)

Every college basketball player wants to win it all,
but, for Rose, playing Duke meant more than just
a chance at the national title. Rose saw Duke as
the embodiment of wealth and privilege that he
was not afforded growing up. To eighteen-year-
old Rose, this privilege seemed antithetical to
his belief in hustling and working hard. He said
in his *30 for 30* documentary that he believed
that programs like Duke did not recruit kids like
him. (*Courtesy of the Bentley Historical Library,
University of Michigan*)

Michigan ultimately lost to Duke 51–71 in the national championship game, but not without a fight. Rose played the loud, aggressive style of basketball he was known for. After an electric start to the second half, Duke scored on several straight possessions, pulling away with a twenty-point lead. Rose had a tremendous game, scoring eighteen second-half points. The game went down in history as a good team losing to a better team, but it only fueled Michigan's five freshmen to come back next April even stronger. (*Courtesy of the Bentley Historical Library, University of Michigan*)

By the end of Jalen Rose's freshman campaign, he had already secured the title of Michigan icon. In the 1991–1992 season, Rose averaged 17.6 points per game, which made him the team's leading scorer as a freshman and setting the school scoring record for freshmen. Rose also became nationally recognized for his bold personality on and off the court. His charm and public appeal cemented the Fab 5's identity not just as impressive basketball players, but as pop culture figures. (*Courtesy of the Bentley Historical Library, University of Michigan*)

The summer after the Fab 5's freshman year, Coach Fisher thought it would be a good idea to take the team on a trip abroad and expose them to different cultures. Rose, however, had a different concept of an ideal summer. The Fab 5's Spain trip is marked by Rose's antics. At the time, Fisher was frustrated by Rose and his outspoken nature, but, retrospectively, it's a reminder that Rose was thoroughly himself no matter the circumstances. He was loud, outspoken, and uncontrollable whether on the court or on the streets of Barcelona. (*Courtesy of the Bentley Historical Library, University of Michigan*)

Michigan kicked off the 1992–1993 season with two exhibition games, the first of which was against the Russian national team and the second of which, pictured here, was against Ragnone Attorney AAU. By this point, Rose had already established a reputation for himself—the Michigan Daily's Ken Sugiura inquired in his November 23 article whether Rose could "talk smack in Russian." (*Courtesy of the Bentley Historical Library, University of Michigan*)

In December 1992, Michigan faced Duke in a rematch of the National Championship game. Michigan fell to Duke 68–79, but not without a few choice words. Michigan's freshmen reportedly brought their trash-talking A-game against Duke, telling All-American Bobby Hurley that he could not guard Jalen Rose. Perhaps they were right—pictured here is Rose shooting over Hurley. Rose scored a total of fifteen points in this game against Duke. (*Courtesy of the Bentley Historical Library, University of Michigan*)

Pictured here is Rose in a game against Detroit Mercy. Rose grew up on the west side of Detroit, where he attended Southwestern High School and played under Coach Perry Watson. Rose brought Detroit with him to the University of Michigan in the form of Watson, who was hired as an assistant coach at Michigan, and Chris Webber, Rose's longtime friend and former AAU teammate. Today, Rose gives back to Detroit through Jalen Rose Leadership Academy, a free, open-enrollment charter school Rose cofounded in the same zip code where he grew up. (*Courtesy of the Bentley Historical Library, University of Michigan*)

Pictured here is Rose wearing black socks, which the Fab 5 are often credited for making fashionable. The first time the Fab 5 boys wore black socks for a game, they made sure to keep them covered by their warm-ups until the game started so that Coach Fisher would not have time to tell them to go change. However, by early December, they had converted the rest of the team (save for Eric Riley, Michael Talley, Jason Bossard, and Leon Derricks) into wearing black socks as well. (*Courtesy of the Bentley Historical Library, University of Michigan*)

After beating both Purdue and Wisconsin by double digits, Michigan fell 75–76 to Indiana for its first conference loss. Rose and Jimmy King tied for leading scorer, with each of them posting nineteen points. Even though the game was close through the final seconds, the win was interpreted as a more mature, experienced team coached by Bobby Knight beating the young, immature Fab 5—a narrative that the Fab 5 seemed to carry with them throughout their entire time at Michigan. (*Courtesy of the Bentley Historical Library, University of Michigan*)

Pictured here is Rose in an early February win against Purdue. Rose put up twelve points in this game. By this point, he had earned a reputation as an extremely talented, if a bit volatile and underdeveloped, player. After the Purdue game, Rose said that he felt that Michigan was in control throughout the course of the game. (*Courtesy of the Bentley Historical Library, University of Michigan*)

In this early March home game against Iowa, Jalen Rose put up sixteen points for an 82–73 victory. Michigan was beginning to secure a national reputation, as was evidenced by the audience; those in the seats at Crisler included hip-hop star Hammer, ESPN commentator Dick Vitale, and basketball legend Julius Erving. After the game, Rose said, "It was like Las Vegas, with all the superstars at the game." (*Courtesy of the Bentley Historical Library, University of Michigan*)

Although this picture shows the Spartans visiting Crisler, one of the quintessential Fab 5 tales takes place when Michigan played at the Breslin Center in 1993. Michigan State's student section was particularly rowdy, and Michigan missed an astounding twenty-three free throws. After the game, a group of Michigan players, including Rose, sat on the "S" on the middle of the court, rolled around, and "simulated defecating" on the "S." Many Michigan fans watched in horror, but this level of brashness was what made the Fab 5, especially Jalen, so famous and so fun. (*Courtesy of the Bentley Historical Library, University of Michigan*)

Rose's biggest controversy during his time at Michigan was the "crackhouse incident." In October 1992, immediately prior to his sophomore season, Rose visited a friend in Detroit to play video games. Unbeknownst to Rose, drugs were being stored in the house. After a police raid, Rose was arrested for "loitering where drugs were stored." In March, the story was leaked to the press and Illinois fans ran with it, chanting "CRACKHOUSE!! CRACKHOUSE!" and "JUST SAY NO!" whenever Rose had the ball. Rose used the chants to fuel his adrenaline and scored an impressive twenty-three points. (*Courtesy of the Bentley Historical Library, University of Michigan*)

Pictured here is Rose in a 1993 preseason game against Croatia. Although his teammate and best friend Chris Webber elected to enter the draft after the 1992–1993 season, Jalen Rose decided to stay at Michigan for one more year. Had he entered the draft, Rose likely would have gone in the top ten, but his loyalty to the Fab 5 and his desire to finally win a championship convinced him to stay another year. In Webber's absence, Rose entered the season as the most important player on the roster. (*Courtesy of the Bentley Historical Library, University of Michigan*)

Rose's height and versatility allowed him to play multiple positions in one game, which was a key asset in the absence of Chris Webber. In the preseason game against Croatia, Rose saw time at four different positions. Although Rose was able to showcase his versatility, it was somewhat difficult for him to establish a new identity after spending two years at point guard. After the Croatia game, he told *The Michigan Daily*, "The last two years, I was handling the ball. Now I'm more of a swing player, so I'm just adjusting to the situation." (*Courtesy of the Bentley Historical Library, University of Michigan*)

Above: The Fab 5 boys were infamous for their relentless trash talk on the court, and Rose was the most outspoken of the group. In his bestselling book *Got to Give the People What They Want*, Rose outlines his "Friendly Guide to Trash-Talking", which includes respecting your opponent, being prepared to deal with the consequences, recognizing that nothing is out of bounds, doing your research, and, of course, winning. Many Michigan fans lamented the "disrespectful" nature of the Fab 5 boys' attitude, but their confidence and brashness are what made them so good. (*Courtesy of the Bentley Historical Library, University of Michigan*)

Left: Pictured here is Rose in a late November game against Cleveland State. After overcoming an eight-point first half deficit, Michigan ultimately went away with an 84–71 victory. Rose scored seventeen points, and after the game, he succinctly told the media: "I stunk." Michigan's sloppy first half could be blamed on a number of factors, including Rose's adjustment to his new positions, and the inability of the underclassmen to make up for the loss of Chris Webber. (*Courtesy of the Bentley Historical Library, University of Michigan*)

On December 11, 1993, Jalen Rose faced Duke one last time. Although Michigan lost 73–63, Rose played perhaps one of the best games of his career, putting up thirty-one points (which, notably, was not even his season record). Michigan's rivalry with Duke is one of the most iconic basketball rivalries of the Fab 5 era. (*Courtesy of the Bentley Historical Library, University of Michigan*)

Pictured here, Rose is shooting over Grant Hill. In ESPN's *30 for 30* documentary about the Fab 5, Rose famously and controversially recalled that he considered Duke's Grant Hill to be an "Uncle Tom." He later clarified the statement and acknowledged any insensitivity it may have conveyed, but the statement remains an artifact of the cultural narrative surrounding the two basketball programs. (*Courtesy of the Bentley Historical Library, University of Michigan*)

Pictured here is Rose in Michigan's 1994 Big Ten opener against rival Michigan State. Michigan made a statement with a 75–64 win, and Rose led the team in scoring with twenty-two points. This game was the last one that Rose ever played against Michigan State. Michigan went 3–1 against State when Jalen Rose was on the team. (*Courtesy of the Bentley Historical Library, University of Michigan*)

In January 1994, Michigan beat Ohio State in overtime 86–75. Jalen Rose was the game's highest scorer with twenty-eight points. After sitting for almost four minutes in the second half, Fisher reportedly told Rose "to play like the All-American he was", and Rose did just that. In the postgame press conference Buckeye guard Jamie Skelton explained Michigan's dominance in overtime simply by saying, "Jalen. I can spell his name any time you want me to." (*Courtesy of the Bentley Historical Library, University of Michigan*)

After Webber left for the NBA, Rose was no longer a member of the famous Fab 5; instead, he was just Jalen Rose. Rose still managed to post impressive numbers without Webber, with 19.9 points per game and a total of 625 points, a notable improvement from both his freshman and sophomore seasons. Rose was also recognized as a consensus second-team All-American in 1994—an honor he had not received his freshman or sophomore year. (*Courtesy of the Bentley Historical Library, University of Michigan*)

The 1993–1994 season was, all things considered, a successful season for both the Wolverines and Jalen Rose, despite the loss of Chris Webber. The Wolverines made a solid tournament run, losing in the Elite Eight to Arkansas, the eventual national champions. However, Rose's impressive numbers did not work to boost his draft stock. In Webber's absence, Rose was moved from point guard to wing, a change that Rose believes made him a less distinctive draft prospect. Rose now describes his decision to stay another year to be "dangerous" because of the risk of injury and decreased draft stock. (*Courtesy of the Bentley Historical Library, University of Michigan*)

Above left: In the 1994 NBA draft, Jalen Rose went thirteenth overall to the Denver Nuggets. His bold red pinstripe suit goes down in history as one of the most iconic NBA draft outfits in history—a quintessential Jalen Rose moment. He admits now that he chose to wear red because he thought he was going to be drafted by the Los Angeles Clippers, whose primary team color is red. (*Courtesy of the Bentley Historical Library, University of Michigan*)

Above right: After two years in Denver, Rose was traded to the Indiana Pacers, where he played alongside Reggie Miller and made three consecutive Eastern Conference Finals appearances. In the 1999–2000 season, he led the team in scoring and won the NBA Most Improved Player Award. After six years in Indiana, Rose played for four more NBA teams before retiring in 2007.

In 2007, Rose paid for this billboard on Seven Mile in Detroit to honor the Fab 5. Today, Rose works as a co-host of *Get Up!*, a morning sports talk show on ESPN, and a co-host of *Jalen and Jacoby* a sports radio show on ESPN Radio. In 2011, Rose produced ESPN's highest-rated *30 for 30* documentary on the Fab 5, which provided a controversial look into Rose's time at Michigan. In 2015, Rose published a memoir, *Got to Give the People What They Want*, which became a *New York Times* bestseller.

3
JUWAN HOWARD

A.K.A. JUWAN ANTONIO HOWARD

BORN: 7 February 1973, Chicago, Illinois
POSITION: Power forward/center
HEIGHT: 6 feet 9 inches
WEIGHT: 250 pounds
JERSEY NUMBER(S): 42 (HS); 25 (UM); 5, 7, 55, 6 (NBA)
HIGH SCHOOL: Chicago Vocational, Chicago, IL
COLLEGE: University of Michigan (1991–1994)

NBA: Washington Bullets/Wizards (1994–2001); Dallas Mavericks (2001–2002; 2007–2008); Denver Nuggets (2002–2003; 2008); Orlando Magic (2003–2004); Houston Rockets (2004–2007); Charlotte Bobcats (2008–2009); Portland Trail Blazers (2009–2010); Miami Heat (2010–2013)

COACHING: assistant, Miami Heat (2013–2019); head, University of Michigan (2019–present)

HIGH SCHOOL HONORS: All-Public League second team (1989); All-Public League first team (1990–1991); Most Valuable Player, Boston Shootout (1990); Illinois Player of the Year (1991); Parade All-American (1990); McDonald's All-American (1990); Gatorade Circle of Champions' Illinois Player of the Year (1990)

COLLEGE HONORS: Two-time NCAA Tournament Runner-up (1992, 1993, vacated); Associated Press third-team All-American (1994); National Association of Basketball Coaches second-team All-American (1994) Elite Eight Most Valuable Player (1994)

PROFESSIONAL HONORS: Two-time NBA Champion (2012, 2013) NBA All-Rookie Second Team (1995); All-NBA Third team (1996); NBA All-Star (1996)

CAREER AVERAGES (PER GAME)

LEVEL	POINTS	REBOUNDS	ASSISTS	STEALS	BLOCKS
College (3 yrs)	15.3	7.5	2.0	0.8	0.6
NBA (19 yrs)	13.4	6.1	2.2	0.7	0.3

Shown here before his freshman season at Michigan, Juwan Howard's life is a story of overcoming adversity. His grandmother Jannie was the daughter of sharecroppers from Belzoni, Mississippi. Juwan was not close to his parents, yet was raised, along with two cousins, by his grandmother. He grew up on the South Side of Chicago, where his grandmother managed to instill values and a work ethic into him that would both keep him out of trouble and allow him to flourish. (*Courtesy of the Bentley Historical Library, University of Michigan*)

Howard would go on to Chicago Vocational Career Academy, which is now simply known as Chicago Vocational High School. There, he was named a member of the academic National Honors Society and was elected the school's homecoming king. Vocational had no heat in their gym, and, in fact, lacked a locker room, forcing players to change in a history classroom. Howard, however, dominated on the court, taking his team as far as the Chicago Public School semifinals. (*Courtesy of the Bentley Historical Library, University of Michigan*)

In his senior year of high school, Howard led his team to a 25–5 record and an appearance in the semifinals of the Chicago Public League tournament. For the season, Howard would average 26.9 points, 8.4 rebounds, and 3.4 assists, all while finishing in the top ten percent of his class academically. He would be named to *Parade* magazine's All-American team and was named all-state in the AA Division for Illinois. He would play for the first time with Michigan teammate Chris Webber in the McDonald's All-American game, putting up sixteen points for a West squad that won 108–106. (*Courtesy of the Bentley Historical Library, University of Michigan*)

Howard accomplished this in spite of a moment of personal tragedy. On the morning November 2, 1990, Howard announced his intention to play basketball at the University of Michigan. A few hours later, Howard arrived home to find that his grandmother had passed away from a massive heart attack. The combined efforts of his high school coach Richard Cook and his future Michigan coaches Steve Fisher and Brian Dutcher helped Howard navigate this tough period in his life, and soon, he was off to Ann Arbor. (*Courtesy of the Bentley Historical Library, University of Michigan*)

This photo shows Juwan Howard leading his Michigan teammates during his freshman season, during a 1.5-mile training run. Basketball, as a sport, requires plenty of running, as evidenced by the average of 2.72 miles that are run in a game by an NBA player. While the run here covers a distance of 1.5 miles (the length of Charlotte Motor Speedway, a standard for race tracks in America), the distance ran in a game is almost twice that, or a little over the distance of Talladega Superspeedway, the longest oval track in the United States. (*Courtesy of the Bentley Historical Library, University of Michigan*)

Before the regular season could get underway, the men's and women's teams of the University of Michigan played an exhibition game each against the Cuban national teams at Crisler Arena. The men won their game by a tally of 84–63. Howard started this game, being the only member of the Fab 5 to do so. He is shown here with coach Steve Fisher, who made him the first recruit in the Fab 5 class, and Eric Riley, who became a consistent sixth man, and went on to NBA glory himself. (*Courtesy of the Bentley Historical Library, University of Michigan*)

Coach Fisher is all smiles as he speaks to Juwan Howard later in the game. Despite some early turnover issues, the Wolverines were never in serious trouble against the Cubans, and the game was never really in doubt. Fisher did a masterful coaching job with the Fab 5, balancing the talent of his young stars with the experience on his squad and their need to learn as they played. Not only did he manage to keep his squad intact, but he managed to set many of his players up for later success in their lives. Howard, for example, has followed his footsteps into coaching. (*Courtesy of the Bentley Historical Library, University of Michigan*)

This photo shows Juwan Howard rising for a dunk during the University of Michigan's game at Crisler Arena, on Monday, December 9, 1991, against Chicago State University. The Wolverines would dominate their non-conference foe, winning by a score of 112–62. Howard would play a key role in Michigan's early efforts on this night, putting up twelve points (on six of seven shooting), eight rebounds, three assists, and an astounding six blocked shots. He did all of this in just twenty-one minutes, while only committing two fouls. (*Courtesy of the Bentley Historical Library, University of Michigan*)

This game was the third in the season for the Wolverines, and Howard had mixed results in the two priors. In the season opener against Detroit Mercy, Howard had scored thirteen points, pulled down nine rebounds, dished out two assists, and blocked a shot in twenty-six minutes, before fouling out. Michigan won 100–74. Against Cleveland State, Howard struggled, scoring two points (on one of seven shooting), pulled down four rebounds, and had one assists and one block in twenty-seven minutes. Despite his struggles, Michigan took home a comfortable win of 80–61. (*Courtesy of the Bentley Historical Library, University of Michigan*)

Up next for the Wolverines, after they handled
Eastern Michigan (91–77) behind a solid game
from Howard—eleven points, ten rebounds (his
first career double-double), and four assists in
twenty-eight minutes—was a showdown with the
top-ranked Duke Blue Devils. This game was a
part of a fierce Duke–Michigan rivalry, which has
seen the erstwhile opponents play thirty times.
Duke leads the series by a tally of 22–8, with the
last game between the two stalwarts being played
on December 3, 2013. That game was won by
Duke, by a tally of 73–69. (*Courtesy of the Bentley
Historical Library, University of Michigan*)

Aside from Big Ten teams, and intrastate rivals
from Michigan, the Wolverines have played Duke
more than any other team in their history. Twice
(thanks to the NCAA tournament), the squads
have played each other twice in the same season:
2008–2009, 1963–1964, and this season, Juwan's
freshman season, 1991–1992. There would be
games between members of the Fab 5 and Duke
every year the group had a player in school, as a
part of a longer run of games between 1989 and
2000. (*Courtesy of the Bentley Historical Library,
University of Michigan*)

This particular game was one of the best of the series. Duke, the defending national champions, boasted six players that would later go on to NBA success (Christian Laettner, Grant Hill, Bobby Hurley, Cherokee Parks, Brian Davis, and Antonio Lang), with two more who were drafted yet played professionally elsewhere (Eric Meek and Thomas Hill). Shown here on defense, Howard would often be matched up with Laettner, who would go on to both be named national player of the year, and to play for the 1992 Dream Team, the only collegiate player to do so. (*Courtesy of the Bentley Historical Library, University of Michigan*)

This photo shows Howard gathering in one of his eight rebounds against the Blue Devils. Although he played a stellar game on the boards, the rest of the game was rough going for Juwan, as he scored only four points (on 1–5 shooting), with two assists, one block, and a dismal six turnovers. In spite of his subpar performance, the young Wolverines went toe-to-toe with the national champs, forcing the game to overtime before losing 88–85. The two teams would, for only the third time, play each other again that season, but the second game featured much higher stakes. (*Courtesy of the Bentley Historical Library, University of Michigan*)

Michigan would enter the tournament 20–8, with an 11–7 record in the Big Ten. This was only good enough for a six seed. Personally, Juwan would finish the season with a stat line of 11.1 points, 6.2 rebounds, 1.8 assists, 0.4 steals, and 0.6 blocks, while averaging 28.1 minutes per game. Their low seed aside, the Wolverines would make it all the way to the national championship game, where a rematch with Duke awaited. The upstart Michigan squad actually led 31–30 at halftime, but the experience and depth of the Duke squad proved to be too much, as the Blue Devils would pull away to win 71–51. Howard had nine points and three rebounds in the final. (*Courtesy of the Bentley Historical Library, University of Michigan*)

This photo shows Juwan Howard before the start of his sophomore year for the Michigan Wolverines, 1992–1993. Howard would improve on his stellar freshman season, as the Fab 5 coalesced as a unit and became a national phenomenon. As the revenue from the basketball team nearly doubled, Howard put together another stellar season, averaging 14.6 points, 7.4 rebounds, 1.9 assists, 0.6 steals, and 0.4 blocks, while averaging a robust 30.1 minutes per game. He did all this while majoring in communications (a degree he would finish in 1995) and spending time making trips to visit the sick at the University of Michigan hospital. (*Courtesy of the Bentley Historical Library, University of Michigan*)

This photo shows Juwan Howard trying to make a layup off the glass against Detroit Mercy, at Crisler Arena, during the team's game on Monday, December 7, 1992. The Wolverines had opened the season 1–1, with a road win against Rice and a loss on the road to defending national champions Duke. Sixth-ranked Michigan would win this game 92–77, the start of an eleven-game winning streak. Howard, for his part, would finish with sixteen points and seven rebounds in just twenty-two minutes of game time. (*Courtesy of the Bentley Historical Library, University of Michigan*)

The Wolverines would go on to beat Bowling Green in their next game by a tally of 79–68. Howard would contribute twelve points, four rebounds, and one assist in thirty-three minutes of game time. This left the Michigan squad at 3–1 heading into their matchup with Cleveland State. Knowing that, with his improved play, he would be a top prospect in the NBA, Howard wisely decided to take out an NCAA-approved insurance policy through the Exceptional Student Athlete Disability Insurance Program that would pay him $1 million in the event of a career-ending injury. (*Courtesy of the Bentley Historical Library, University of Michigan*)

As for the game against Cleveland State? It was one of Howard's finest performances of the season. In just twenty-five minutes of game action, Howard put up a season-high twenty-one points. This impressive scoring total was augmented by eleven rebounds, one assist, and two blocked shots. Juwan did this on an impressive 75 percent shooting, while going nine from eleven from the free throw line. All was well in Wolverine land, as the Fab 5 led the team to an 88–56 win over Cleveland State, improving their season record to four wins, one loss. (*Courtesy of the Bentley Historical Library, University of Michigan*)

After a win over Iowa State, the 5–1 Michigan squad would move on to play Central Michigan, and not even a high-five to the face by an unidentified Chippewas player could slow Howard and the Fab 5 down. Michigan would improve to 6–1 by smashing Central Michigan by a tally of 94–69. In thirty-one minutes of game action, Juwan would score sixteen points, grab five rebounds, and dish out two assists, with two steals to boot. He was a perfect four of four from the charity stripe. This was the fifth win in an eleven-game winning streak. (*Courtesy of the Bentley Historical Library, University of Michigan*)

On Tuesday, January 26, 1993, Juwan Howard and the Michigan Fab 5 would play their first of two games against their biggest rival, the Ohio State Buckeyes. Michigan entered the game with a stellar 16–2 record, ranked no. 5 in the country, and did not disappoint. Michigan would topple the Buckeyes at Crisler Arena by a score of 72–62, extending their current winning streak to four games. Juwan Howard would score fourteen points, grab six rebounds, dish out four assists, and block one shot in thirty-one minutes of game time. (*Courtesy of the Bentley Historical Library, University of Michigan*)

On Sunday, February 7, 1993, the seventh-ranked Michigan Wolverines, led by Juwan Howard and the Fab 5, would host the nineteenth-ranked Purdue Boilermakers at Crisler Arena. Michigan, with a record of 18–3 headed into this matchup, would take their second win of the season over Purdue by a tally of 84–76. Along with his Fab 5 brethren, Howard led the way, scoring eighteen points, ripping down seventeen boards, and even managing an assist in thirty-five minutes of game time. This was the second of a three-game winning streak. (*Courtesy of the Bentley Historical Library, University of Michigan*)

On Sunday, February 28, 1993, Juwan Howard and the fifth-ranked Michigan Wolverines travelled to Columbus for their second matchup of the season against the Buckeyes of Ohio State University. Although a struggle, the Fab 5, Juwan Howard, and Michigan would emerge with a 66–64 win. The win would move the Wolverines to a 22–4 mark on the season. Howard played a monster game, scoring eighteen points while grabbing an incredible sixteen rebounds, which were crucial in this defensive struggle. He also provided three assists and a blocked shot. (*Courtesy of the Bentley Historical Library, University of Michigan*)

On Sunday, March 7, 1993, the hated Michigan State Spartans would travel to Ann Arbor for a matchup with the fourth-ranked Michigan Wolverines. Michigan would complete a season sweep of the Spartans that day, winning by an overtime tally of 87–81. Playing thirty-seven grueling minutes, Juwan Howard was a key contributor to victory that day, scoring nineteen points, pulling down seven rebounds, and dishing out two assists, to go along with two steals, before he fouled out of the contest. (*Courtesy of the Bentley Historical Library, University of Michigan*)

Shown here after his playing days showing off a Michigan warm up jacket, Juwan Howard and the rest of the Fab 5 faced a daunting task heading into the 1993–1994 season. Fab 5 member and All-American Chris Webber had left for the NBA. The team had lost the national championship game in heartbreaking fashion the season prior, yet there were still high expectations for Howard and the Wolverines. Howard put up an amazing campaign, averaging 20.8 points, 8.9 rebounds, 2.4 assists, 1.5 steals, and 0.7 blocks in thirty-four minutes per game. He would be named a third-team All-American.

The year prior, the nationally-ranked Wolverines had lost an embarrassing preseason game to an AAU team sponsored by Sam Rangone, attorney, by a tally of 122–121. Howard and the Wolverines exacted their revenge by beating the upstarts on Monday, November 22, 1993, by a score of 112–82. Howard would, in just twenty-six minutes, put up twenty-two points, pull down fourteen rebounds, and dish out two assists, on ten of thirteen shooting. The result was a sign of good things to come for Howard and the Wolverines. (*Courtesy of the Bentley Historical Library, University of Michigan*)

After starting the season with a no. 5 ranking and an 80–70 win over no. 13 Georgia Tech, the Wolverines would play long time non-conference foe Cleveland State at Crisler Arena. The Howard-led Wolverines would dominate both ends of the floor, winning by a tally of 84–71. Howard, for his part, continued his dominance of Cleveland State. In thirty-five minutes, Howard put up twenty-five points, pulled down twelve boards, dished out two assists, and added three steals and three blocks. With the win, Michigan moved to 2–0 on the season. (*Courtesy of the Bentley Historical Library, University of Michigan*)

Michigan would move on to play Tennessee-Chattanooga at home on Saturday, December 4, 1993 at Crisler Arena. The game would be a high-scoring affair, one that was much closer than anticipated, with the Wolverines beating the now-Mockingbirds by a score of 97–86. A member of that Mockingbirds squad was Terrell Owens, who would go on to much greater success in the NFL, where he would play for fourteen seasons as a member of the 49ers, Eagles, Cowboys, Bills, and Bengals, making the Pro Football Hall of Fame in 2018. (*Courtesy of the Bentley Historical Library, University of Michigan*)

Famous benchwarmers aside, Juwan Howard, along with his Fab 5 teammates, helped lead the Wolverines to another win. In the matchup against Tennessee–Chattanooga, Howard would score twenty-two points, pull down eight rebounds, offer up two assists, and make one steal, all in the course of thirty-six minutes. Juwan, however, would miss Michigan's next game, a 78–60 win over Detroit Mercy, after straining his Achilles tendon in the practice following the Chattanooga game. It would be one of two games that Howard missed on the season. (*Courtesy of the Bentley Historical Library, University of Michigan*)

Howard would return for the team's loss to Duke (a game where, in thirty-eight minutes, he would score twenty points and nab six rebounds) before leading the seventh-ranked Wolverines onto the floor against intrastate rival Central Michigan. Howard would see limited action in the game, putting in just fifteen minutes during the Wolverines 86–44 demolishing of Central Michigan. In that short space, Howard scored eleven points, pulled down five rebounds, and blocked one shot, all on 62.5 percent shooting. (*Courtesy of the Bentley Historical Library, University of Michigan*)

After the win over the Chippewas, the next three non-conference games would prep Howard and the Wolverines for Big Ten play. In a 102–81 neutral-court win over Auburn, Howard would, in twenty-seven minutes, score twenty points, pull down four rebounds, make one assist, and come up with three steals. In a 119–95 loss to twelfth-ranked Arizona, Howard would have twenty points, eleven rebounds, and three assists in thirty-one minutes of action. Howard and Michigan would rebound with a 111–84 win over Boston University. Howard had nineteen points, six rebounds, five assists, and three steals in thirty-two minutes. (*Courtesy of the Bentley Historical Library, University of Michigan*)

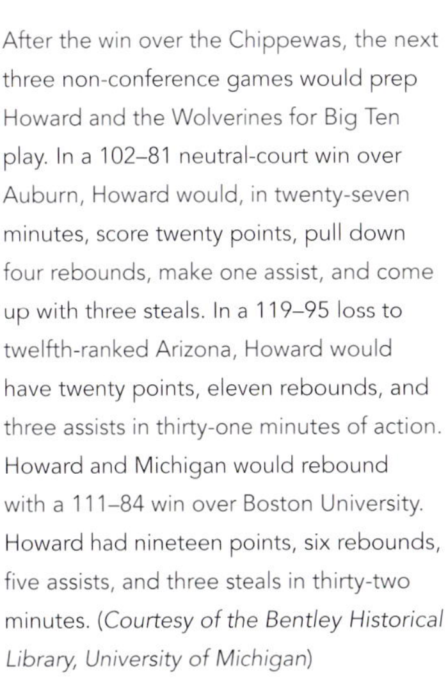

The Wolverines would kick off Big Ten play with a home matchup against their interstate rivals, the Michigan State Spartans. With the game taking place on Wednesday, January 5, 1994, the Wolverines would come up big, knocking the Spartans off by a score of 74–64. For his part, Howard would put up seventeen points, six rebounds, three assists, a steal, and two blocked shots in thirty-four minutes of action. The win would improve the Wolverines to 9–2 and would be the second in a four-game winning streak. (*Courtesy of the Bentley Historical Library, University of Michigan*)

In the first of two matchups against heated rivals Ohio State, the Wolverines would, on Thursday, January 13, 1994, pull off an 86–82 victory over the Buckeyes at Crisler Arena. Howard was a big part of the Wolverines' effort on that day, scoring nineteen points and coming up with a double-double after snagging his tenth rebound. He would also have two assists, two steals, and a blocked shot. The win would move the Wolverines to a 11–2 mark on the season, which included a 3–0 start in Big Ten play. (*Courtesy of the Bentley Historical Library, University of Michigan*)

On Saturday, January 29, 1993, the thirteenth-ranked Wolverines faced a tough task, going head-to-head with the nineteenth-ranked Wisconsin Badgers. In a must-win Big Ten matchup, the Wolverines managed to eke out a 79–75 win over Wisconsin. The win improved the Wolverines record to 13–4 on the season. Howard, for his part, scored twenty-two points, pulled down eight rebounds, dished out an assist, came up with two steals, and blocked one shot. He managed all of this in thirty-seven grueling minutes. (*Courtesy of the Bentley Historical Library, University of Michigan*)

Saturday, February 4, 1994, saw the Wolverines travel to the Breslin Events Center on the campus of Michigan State, in East Lansing, Michigan, to take on the hated Spartans. In a defensive struggle, the thirteenth-ranked Wolverines came out on top of their heated, yet unranked, rivals, by a score of 59–51. Juwan Howard (pictured here in the teams' first matchup of the season), helped lead the way for Michigan, tallying a double-double with eighteen points, twelve rebounds, three assists, and a blocked shot. Michigan improved to 15–5 on the season. (*Courtesy of the Bentley Historical Library, University of Michigan*)

After his junior season, an Elite Eight berth, and a third-team All-American nod, Howard would declare early for the NBA draft, where he would be the no. 5 overall pick by the then Washington Bullets, which would later become the Washington Wizards. Here, he would be reunited with Fab 5 classmate Chris Webber, who had arrived in Washington via trade before the start of Howard's rookie season. The two would spend parts of four seasons together, although injuries and coaching would prevent them from replicating their success in Ann Arbor.

In all, Howard would spend seven seasons in Washington, becoming the name and the face of a franchise where he would be awarded the first $100-million contract in NBA history, His time in Washington was productive, as he made the 1995 all-rookie team, the 1996 All-Star team, and the 1996 All-NBA third team. As a Wizard, Howard averaged 18.4 points, 7.4 rebounds, 3.3 assists, a steal, and 0.3 blocks per game. The Wizards would make the playoffs once in Howard's tenure, where they were swept by Michael Jordan and the Bulls.

After season-long stints with the Mavericks (where he would make his second playoff appearance), Nuggets, and Magic, Howard would find himself traded to the Houston Rockets in a seven-player deal. He would return to the playoffs in Houston, twice making it to the first round. As a Rocket, Howard averaged 10.4 points, 6.1 rebounds, 1.5 assists, 0.5 steals, and 0.1 blocks per game across three seasons, although he would be hampered by an MCL injury and a severe viral infection.

It would take the final two years of his career for Howard to become the first Fab 5 member to win a championship beyond the high school level. After second stints with Dallas and Denver, followed by time spent with Charlotte and Portland, Howard signed, as a free agent, with the Miami Heat, at the same time as LeBron James and Chris Bosh. Although the Heat fell to Dallas in the NBA finals in Howard's first season, the Heat would go on to win back-to-back championships with Howard, who played little, serving as a mentor. Howard was on the floor when the Heat clinched the 2012 NBA Championship.

This rather candid photograph shows Juwan Howard mentoring a very young Dwight Howard. Although to say that Juwan is responsible for Dwight's success would be a reach, there is little doubt that the experience imparted by Howard would go on to help Dwight. Dwight has been named to eight all-star teams, eight all-NBA teams, and four NBA all-defensive teams. He was also named the NBA Defensive Player of the Year three times and has led the league in rebounds five times. Dwight has a gold medal in men's basketball and won the NBA Slam Dunk Contest in 2008.

Shortly after leaving the game as a player, Pat Riley, Erik Spoelstra, and the Miami Heat front office named Howard an assistant coach, starting with the 2013 season. That year, Howard helped coach the Heat back to the NBA Finals, before the departures of LeBron James and Chris Bosh marked the end of a dynasty. In that time, Miami has managed a record of 263–229, with three division titles, three playoff berths, and one trip to the NBA finals. On May 22, 2019, Juwan Howard was named the head coach of his alma mater, the University of Michigan Wolverines.

4
JIMMY KING

A.K.A. JIMMY HAL KING

BORN: 9 August 1973, South Bend, Indiana

POSITION: Shooting guard

HEIGHT: 6 feet 5 inches

WEIGHT: 210 pounds

JERSEY NUMBER(S): 24 (HS); 24 (UM); 24, 13 (NBA)

HIGH SCHOOL: Plano East, Plano, TX

COLLEGE: University of Michigan (1991–1995)

NBA: Toronto Raptors (1995–1996); Denver Nuggets (1997)

OTHER PROFESSIONAL: Quad City Thunder [Continental Basketball Association] (1996–2000); La Crosse Bobcats [CBA] (1999–2000); Sioux City Skyforce [CBA] (2000); Gary Steelheads [CBA] (2000–2001); Great Lakes Storm [CBA] (2003–2004); Asheville Attitude [NBA-G] (2001–2002); Texas Tycoons [American Basketball Association] (2004–2005); Trotamundos B. B. C. [Venezuela] (2001); Guaiqueries de Margarita [Venezuela] (2005); Spojnia Stargard Szczecinski [Poland] (2002–2003).

COACHING: Head, Ecourse Community High School (2016–2018).

HIGH SCHOOL HONORS: *Parade* All-American, Second Team (1990); McDonald's All-American (1990); Mr. Basketball, Texas (1990).

COLLEGE HONORS: Two-time NCAA Tournament Runner-up (1992, 1993, vacated).

PROFESSIONAL HONORS: Drafted in the second round (thirty-fifth) by the Toronto Raptors in the 1995 NBA Draft; CBA Champion (1998); CBA Most Valuable Player (1998); Bronze medal, 1998 FIBA World Championships (Team USA).

CAREER AVERAGES (PER GAME)

LEVEL	POINTS	REBOUNDS	ASSISTS	STEALS	BLOCKS
College (4 yrs)	11.9	4.1	2.7	1.4	0.3
NBA (2 yrs)	4.5	1.8	1.4	0.4	0.2

Jimmy King grew up in Plano, Texas, where he began setting lofty goals for his basketball career at a young age. As the top-ranked shooting guard in his recruiting class, King received offers from several of the top programs in the country, eventually narrowing it down to Notre Dame, Kansas, and Michigan. He met Juwan Howard during their recruiting visit at Michigan, and the two quickly became friends. Howard ended up being one of the most persuasive forces convincing King to choose Michigan. (*Courtesy of the Bentley Historical Library, University of Michigan*)

King was the second member of Fisher's prized Fab 5 recruiting class to commit to Michigan. After arriving to campus, the five freshmen, who were unapologetically aware of their basketball prowess, quickly began to clash with the upperclassmen, who felt they had paid their dues over the years and therefore earned starting roles. In one instance, Jimmy King found himself in a small fight with Jason Bossard, a sophomore guard who knocked King to the ground and shouted, "I don't give a shit who you are! I've been here two years, and you just got here." (*Courtesy of the Bentley Historical Library, University of Michigan*)

Even though King was the top shooting guard in his recruiting class, at the beginning of the season, he and Ray Jackson were the only two freshmen not included in the starting lineup. Despite this, King was still an immediate contributor. Pictured here is a dunk against Chicago State in early December, where King played seventeen minutes and finished with eleven points and four rebounds. After the game, Fisher pointed to King's increasing comfort on the court as one of Michigan's assets. (*Courtesy of the Bentley Historical Library, University of Michigan*)

By the end of the 1991 calendar year, Michigan was 8–1, and the Fab 5 boys had caught the nation's attention. On December 14, the young Wolverines forced the reigning national champions, the Duke Blue Devils, into overtime. Although Michigan ultimately came short of a win, the freshman core proved that it could hold its own against one of the best teams in the country. After losing to Duke, Michigan won four straight games to close out non-conference play. (*Courtesy of the Bentley Historical Library, University of Michigan*)

By the time Big Ten play opened in January, King had cracked the starting lineup and proven himself to be a serious contributor, but not without room for improvement. Pictured here is King with juniors Rob Pelinka and Eric Riley in a game against Illinois, where King played for fifteen minutes for a total of three fouls and three points. Prior to the Illinois game, Michigan had lost two consecutive Big Ten games, and the errors were attributed to the inexperience of the team's young core. Eyes turned to Steve Fisher to coach his freshmen into a more disciplined game. (*Courtesy of the Bentley Historical Library, University of Michigan*)

The lack of maturity among Michigan's starting lineup proved a major liability in Big Ten play. After an eighteen-point loss to Wisconsin, which was a particularly poor game for Jimmy King, Michigan traveled to Columbus to take on the Ohio State Buckeyes on March 3. Prior to the game, King found that he and Ray Jackson had lost their starting spots to upperclassmen James Voskuil and Michael Talley. King still played for twenty-six minutes and scored ten points, but it was not enough for the Wolverines, who fell to Ohio State for the second time that season.

Just a few days after losing to Ohio State, Michigan beat Bobby Knight's Indiana Hoosiers 68–60. After the game, King said he had to remind himself not to do what he did at Ohio State, and he seemed to have learned his lesson. King scored eighteen points, including ten in the first seven minutes, making him the team's leading scorer. After the game, Coach Fisher said that King was "sensational" in the first half. The Indiana win was particularly important because it likely secured Michigan's spot in the NCAA tournament.

Above: Michigan was projected to go into the tournament as no. 3 or no. 4 seed, so when the bracket was released and Michigan was no. 6 seed, many saw it as a snub. Before the tournament, the team met with Muhammad Ali, who instructed them to "shock the world." This catchphrase became the team's *de facto* motto throughout the tournament. Michigan beat Temple 73–66 in the first round and became the first team to start five freshmen in the history of the NCAA tournament.

Left: In the second round, Michigan beat East Tennessee State 102–90, and the five freshmen received all the credit as they scored eighty-eight of the team's 102 points and played over 150 of the team's 200 minutes. After the game, Fisher complimented the two guards—Rose and King—for their decision-making. King played arguably one of his best games yet, performing with a level of creativity and excitement that fans had not seen before. A couple weeks later, in the Final Four, King was instrumental to the Wolverines' success, leading the team in scoring with seventeen points.

Pictured here is (from left to right) Juwan Howard, Chris Webber, Jalen Rose, and Jimmy King—four-fifths of the Fab 5. During the 1991–1992 season, the greatest recruiting class of all time proved that they were more than just hype. The season ultimately ended with a 51–71 loss to Duke in the National Championship game. King played for almost the entire game, but the Blue Devils held him to only seven points, a performance that would fuel him to improve for next season.

King's freshman campaign proved to be a success by almost every indicator. As a freshman, he averaged 9.9 points per game, shot 49.6 percent from the field, led the team in three-point percentage (46.7 percent), and started for the majority of conference and postseason play, including the NCAA National Championship game. Although he did not receive as much media attention as Chris Webber or Jalen Rose, he was one of the most important members of the team and was recognized for his leaping ability and flashy dunks.

The start of the 1992–1993 season marked a new era for the Fab 5 boys. First of all, they were not freshmen anymore. Second, they were no longer the hyped young recruiting class; instead, they were established college basketball players with a full year of experience under their belts. Third, and perhaps most important, they wore black socks. King was expected to start at shooting guard, and fans eagerly waited to see how his game had improved in the offseason. (*Courtesy of the Bentley Historical Library, University of Michigan*)

Off the court, King might not have been the most outspoken player on the roster, but on the court, he often excited the fans with electric dunks. Pictured here is a dunk in a preseason exhibition game against Ragnone Attorney AAU, in which Michigan truly "shocked the world" by losing in overtime. The players claimed that the loss was not an indication of how the season would pan out, but the narrative from the previous season persisted as fans and media members complained about the team's "immature" and "undisciplined" playing style. (*Courtesy of the Bentley Historical Library, University of Michigan*)

For the season opener, the team traveled to King's home state of Texas to take on the Rice Owls. Michigan won 75–71, and King scored nine points. Perhaps most importantly, the Fab 5 boys debuted the iconic black socks that would subsequently become standard basketball attire. Pictured here: King v. Ragnone Attorney AAU (*Courtesy of the Bentley Historical Library, University of Michigan*)

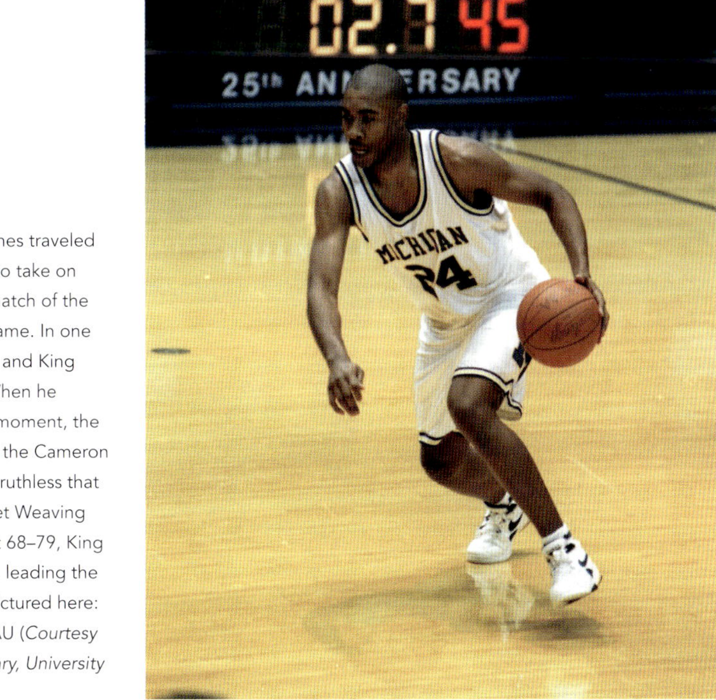

On December 5, the Wolverines traveled to Cameron Indoor Stadium to take on the Duke Blue Devils in a rematch of the 1992 NCAA championship game. In one instance, the net got tangled and King volunteered to untangle it. When he struggled untangling it for a moment, the Duke fans, who are known as the Cameron Crazies and were particularly ruthless that night, began chanting "Basket Weaving 101!" Although Michigan lost 68–79, King had himself an electric game, leading the offense with twenty points. Pictured here: King v. Ragnone Attorney AAU (*Courtesy of the Bentley Historical Library, University of Michigan*)

Pictured here is King taking direction from Coach Fisher during the 1992–1993 home opener against Detroit Mercy. Although the game was rather lackluster at the get-go, Michigan ultimately pulled through with a 92–77 win. King was 3–6 from the field, with a total of six points, three assists, and one foul. After the game, Coach Fisher said that the team needed to improve on everything, especially on the defensive end. (*Courtesy of the Bentley Historical Library, University of Michigan*)

Although King had been an All-American in high school, his numbers his freshman and sophomore years of college did not always reflect the potential he had shown as a recruit. However, in an early February game against Purdue, King gave the fans a flash of promise. He went ten for eleven from the field and three for three from the line for a total of twenty-four points, in addition to six rebounds, three blocks, and three steals. This game marked the fourth time in his Michigan career that he led the team in scoring, but it certainly would not be the last.

Pictured here is King celebrating after Michigan's first round win against Coastal Carolina in the 1993 NCAA tournament. Michigan was given no. 1 seed this year and secured fairly easy first and second round wins before beating UCLA in a nail-biting Sweet Sixteen game. Due to upsets in the first two rounds, Michigan had a fairly easy path to the Final Four, where they beat Kentucky in overtime. Throughout the tournament, King showed that he had developed into a strong two-way player.

The last game that the Fab 5 played together was the National Championship against UNC. It resulted in a heartbreaking loss, but King played as hard as he had all season, with a total of fifteen points, two fouls, four assists, and one rebound. His intensity was evident, but his shots just were not falling, and he only went 6–13 from the field.

His sophomore year, Jimmy King averaged 10.8 points per game, 4.4 rebounds, and 3.1 assists, a remarkable improvement from his freshman year. He finished the season as ninth in the Big Ten for two-point field goal percentage, assists, and true shooting percentage.

King was one of the more reserved members of the Fab 5, but during his sophomore season, he quietly developed into one of the team's best all-around players. Chris Webber entered the NBA draft in 1993, meaning that the Wolverines were left without their leading scorer. This left King, who entered the season as the team's leading field goal shooter at 50.9 percent, as one of the most important remaining players on the roster. King's versatility would also prove vital, as Fisher could place him in both the one- and two-guard positions.

Pictured here is a Jimmy King dunk against Duke during his junior year, the first year post Fab 5. Although Michigan lost to Duke for the third consecutive year, it was clear that the once young and undisciplined core had matured significantly. King, Jackson, Rose, Howard, and sophomore Dugan Fife were the clear leaders of the team, and King, Rose, and Howard, consistently posted double-digit scoring numbers.

In the 1993–1994 season, King averaged 12.3 points, 3.8 rebounds, and 2.6 assists—another steady improvement from the year prior. He finished top ten in the Big Ten for a two-point shooting percentage and steals per game. At the end of the season, Juwan Howard and Jalen Rose would head to the NBA draft, leaving King and Ray Jackson as the only Fab 5 players to return to Michigan for their senior years. (*Courtesy of the Bentley Historical Library, University of Michigan*)

King's game earned him due respect among the rest of the Fab 5 boys, but according to Mitch Albom's book, his upbringing in Plano, Texas meant some clear cultural differences between King and his teammates. About 8 percent of the students at the University of Michigan identified as black at the time, which was not a significant shock for King, who grew up in a mostly white community. Howard, Rose, Webber, and Jackson, however, had grown up in majority black communities and often shared tales about the hardships of life in the "hood", all while teasing King for his privileged upbringing. (*Courtesy of the Bentley Historical Library, University of Michigan*)

King used his senior season to prove what a capable leader and strong player he was. He became the eighth player in Michigan history to 1,500 points and 500 rebounds in a career. He averaged 14.7 points, 1.9 steals, and 2.9 assists. He was in the top ten in the Big Ten for field goals, field goal attempts, two-point field goals, two-point field goal attempts, and steals per game.

Pictured here is Jimmy King during a February 1995 game against Wisconsin. Michigan lost 65–70, and King led the team in scoring with twenty points. This loss was a meaningful one for Michigan, who remained on the NCAA tournament bubble after making it to the NCAA championship game the two years prior. Michigan would go 4–3 in its remaining regular season games, securing a spot in the NCAA tournament for the fourth consecutive year.

In the 1995 NBA draft, King went in the second round (35th overall) to the Toronto Raptors. His rookie season, he played sixty-two games, averaging 4.5 points, 1.8 rebounds, and 1.4 assists per game. King had a twenty-year professional basketball career, including several seasons in Europe with the Continental Basketball Association (CBA). In 1998, he was the CBA MVP with the Quad City Thunder. He also played for the U.S. national team in the 1998 FIBA World Championship.

After he retired from professional basketball, King returned to southeast Michigan and remains an active member of the community. Pictured here, King attended the Curtis Granderson third Annual Celebrity Shoot-Out, an event organized by the former Detroit Tiger to raise money for the Grand Kids Foundation. In 2010, King was joined by Jalen Rose and fellow Wolverine and Heisman trophy winner Desmond Howard for a fun evening of basketball and community engagement.

In November 2010, Ray Jackson, Jalen Rose, and Jimmy King returned to Crisler Arena to watch Michigan take on Gardner-Webb in game two of the Legends Classic. At this point, sanctions prevented Webber from associating himself with the university, so a true Fab 5 reunion at Crisler was impossible. However, the return of three Michigan basketball greats was enough to send a spark of excitement through Crisler.

Pictured here is Jimmy King playing at the Braylon Edwards Foundation Celebrity Basketball Tournament at Pioneer High School in Ann Arbor, Michigan, in 2011. King was joined by several other former Michigan athletes, including Denard Robinson, Roy Roundtree, Tim Hardaway, Jr., Jordan Morgan, Mike Martin, Zack Novak, Stu Douglass, David Merritt, and Ronald Bellamy to raise money for the University of Michigan's A. Alfred Taubman Medical Research Institute, for ALS research.

Jimmy King remains an incredibly involved member of the Michigan athletics community. Here he is at the annual Michigan Alumni Flag Football Game in the Big House, an annual event that precedes the spring football game and is coached by notable Michigan football alumni.

In 2013, Michigan made its first NCAA National Championship appearance since the Fab 5 days. Pictured here is Jimmy King, Ray Jackson, and Jalen Rose cheering for Michigan in the stands. Juwan Howard is not pictured but he was standing to King's right. Before the Sweet Sixteen game, King gave a guest lecture to a Culture of Basketball class that included Michigan basketball's current freshman class: Spike Albrecht, Nik Stauskas, Caris LeVert, Mitch McGary, and Glenn Robinson III. King served as a mentor, reminding them to be confident and aggressive throughout the tournament.

In 1991, Jimmy King made an appearance on *Detroit Rubber*, a weekly reality YouTube series produced by Eminem. The show details Burn Rubber, a sneaker shop in metro Detroit that serves as a destination for local celebrities. In the season two premiere, King showed his dedication to the Fab 5 legacy by pitching the idea of a Fab 5 T-shirt line collaboration. Jalen Rose also made a cameo in that episode.

Pictured here is Jimmy King with Juwan Howard at the Fab 5 boys and girls basketball camp. King organized and hosted the camp, and proceeds went to benefit the Flint water crisis, C.S. Mott Children's Hospital, and other charities. King, Howard, Jalen Rose, and Ray Jackson all attended the camp—a testament to their sustained friendship almost twenty-five years after they all played together.

Since retiring from professional basketball, King has remained one of Michigan basketball's most engaged alumni. Pictured here, he is wearing a Michigan hat to show support for his alma mater.

In October 2016, King, Rose, and Jackson participated in a forum at the University of Michigan entitled "Fab Five @ 25: A Public Discussion of a Time, a Team, and Their Legacy." In the forum, King, Rose, and Jackson discussed pertinent issues like racism on campus and whether college athletes should be paid. When it comes to creating a safer environment for students on campus, King said, "That's the reason why we wanted to have this forum, so that we can have this discussion because we have the power to change what's occurring."

In February 2017, King and Ray Jackson spoke in a University of Michigan lecture entitled "The Black Male Athlete. Who Is He & What Is He to You?" The panelists spoke about the stereotypes surrounding black male athletes, particularly at the University of Michigan. King discussed his experiences as a Fab 5 athlete, in which he often felt pressured and exploited: "You don't want to let your community down. You have all this weight on your shoulders … that pressure can break you."

In November 2017, King spoke at Issues and Ale, an event series from Michigan Radio that discusses pertinent issues facing the state of Michigan. Pictured here is King with (from left to right) Michigan Radio's Doug Tribou, sports author John U. Bacon, and sports journalist Joanne Gerstner. The panelists spoke about the intersection of politics and sports, including domestic violence, players kneeling for the national anthem, and paying college athletes.

Pictured here is King embracing longtime friend and teammate Jalen Rose at the Jalen Rose Celebrity Golf Classic, an event that benefits Rose's charter school, Jalen Rose Leadership Academy. Despite fractures in the friendships of the Fab 5 members, Rose and King have remained close friends over the years.

When former teammate Juwan Howard became Michigan basketball's head coach in 2019, King was one of Howard's most vocal supporters. He told Maize n Brew that he sees Howard's coaching position as a part of the Fab 5's legacy: "I think it's a story of the stars aligning, the same way they aligned when we were young All-Americans coming out of high school to form the 'Fab Five.'"

5
RAY
JACKSON

A.K.A. RAY JACKSON, JR.

BORN: 13 November 1973, San Antonio, Texas

POSITION: Shooting guard

HEIGHT: 6'6

WEIGHT: 220 pounds

JERSEY NUMBER(S): 21 (HS); 21 (UM)

HIGH SCHOOL: Lyndon B. Johnson, Austin, TX

COLLEGE: University of Michigan (1991–1995)

PROFESSIONAL: Grand Rapids Mackers/Hoops [Continental Basketball Association] (1996–2001); Trotamundos B. B. C. [Venezuela] (1999); Cocodrilos de Caracas [Venezuela] (2001); Huevla [Spain] (1997–1998); Strasbourg [France] (1997–1998); Obras Sanitarias [Argentina] (1999–2000).

HIGH SCHOOL HONORS: McDonald's All-American (1991).

COLLEGE HONORS: Two-time NCAA Tournament Runner-up (1992, 1993, vacated). Three-time NCAA Elite Eight (1992–1994, vacated). Two-time All Big Ten (1994, 1995).

PROFESSIONAL HONORS: CBA Rookie of the Year; (1995); Venezuelan Champion (1999).

CAREER AVERAGES (PER GAME)

LEVEL	POINTS	REBOUNDS	ASSISTS	STEALS	BLOCKS
College (4 yrs)	10.1	4.6	2.4	1.0	0.3

Ray Jackson was the third member of the Fab 5 recruiting class to commit to Michigan. He grew up in Austin, Texas. Much like the other four members of the Fab 5, he was a local star and began receiving interest from recruiters at a young age. Jackson received several enticing scholarship offers, but he knew all along that he wanted to attend Michigan. He had grown up watching Michigan football, had rooted for Michigan basketball in the 1989 championship game, and now wanted an opportunity to be a part of the best freshman class of all time. (*Courtesy of the Bentley Historical Library, University of Michigan*)

His freshman year, Jackson was the last member of the Fab 5 to start. The season opened with Jalen Rose, Chris Webber, and Juwan Howard as starters, and Jimmy King joined the lineup fairly quickly, but Jackson did not have his first start until February 9. Playing meaningful minutes as a freshman, let alone starting, was a rare feat in the early 1990s, but compared to his fellow "Fab 5" members, Jackson often felt overlooked. Jackson could have been a star at almost any other school, and he later admitted that he considered transferring to be just that. (*Courtesy of the Bentley Historical Library, University of Michigan*)

Michigan was 8–1 going into Big Ten play, but after a double-digit loss to Indiana (pictured here), their conference record was 2–3 in late January. Michigan's freshman core clearly had a lot of talent, but their immaturity and lack of experience was getting the best of them in conference play, and critics wondered if they would qualify for the NCAA tournament. Although Jackson was not yet starting, he was playing significant minutes (seventeen against Indiana) and was a versatile perimeter player who Fisher could rely on as a sub in multiple positions.

By the time the NCAA tournament came around, Jackson was still the member of the Fab 5 who received the least hype and media attention, but he had also earned a consistent spot in the starting lineup and become recognized for his defensive prowess. Pictured here is a Ray Jackson dunk against Cincinnati in the NCAA Final Four. At any other school, Jackson's promise as a freshman would have been the talk of the town, but at Michigan, he often fell into the shadows.

On April 6, 1992, Jackson became one of the first ever freshmen to start in the NCAA National Championship game. In fact, alongside Webber, Rose, Howard, and King, Jackson was a member of the first ever all-freshmen starting lineup in NCAA championship history. Pictured here, Jackson is defending Duke forward Bobby Hurley. Duke ultimately beat Michigan by twenty points (71–51), which many observers painted as a victory of experience over inexperience. Jackson played for sixteen minutes but was held to one rebound, two assists, one foul, and zero points.

Jackson's freshman year was a huge success by most indicators: he played significant minutes and ended the season as a starter on a championship contending team. However, it had also given him an identity he had not been expecting—the "fifth" member of the Fab 5. When he visited home, his friends and family, who had all watched him grow up as a basketball star, constantly asked him why he was not getting more minutes. As Webber, Rose, Howard, and King learned to process their newfound fame, Jackson learned to accept that he did not hold the same celebrity status as his teammates. (*Courtesy of the Bentley Historical Library, University of Michigan*)

In December 1992, the Fab 5 opened their sophomore season wearing black socks. The team traveled to Texas to play Rice, and a friend of Jackson's brought him a pair of black socks from Foot Locker as a gift, and when his fellow starting sophomores saw them, they bought some for themselves as well. The boys wore their sweatpants until right before the game started, so that by the time Coach Fisher saw them, it was too late to make them change. Today, black socks are commonplace in basketball, and Ray Jackson is to thank for that. (*Courtesy of the Bentley Historical Library, University of Michigan*)

Pictured here is Ray Jackson during a December game against Cleveland State. In this game, Jackson played for twelve minutes and scored two points. This game was played at Crisler Arena in Ann Arbor and had an attendance of 12,984.

In late December 1992, Jackson suffered a shoulder injury that forced him to sit out for seven straight games. He returned in January with a newfound spark and was met with a standing ovation in Crisler and postgame praise from teammates Webber and Rose. Michigan Daily columnist Ken Sugiura likened Jackson to a pinky finger—smaller and less notorious than its counterparts, but essential to the function of the hand. (*Courtesy of the Bentley Historical Library, University of Michigan*)

Pictured here is Jackson high-fiving his teammates Juwan Howard and Jalen Rose during an 84–76 win against Purdue. Late in the second half of this game, Jackson turned on his left ankle during a fast break drive and was forced to sit for the rest of the game. During the ten minutes he did play, he made two field goals and two free throws for a total of six points. In his characteristically easy-going fashion, Jackson said after the game, "I'm just doing what I expect myself to do. There's nothing special in that at all." (*Courtesy of the Bentley Historical Library, University of Michigan*)

In March 1993, Michigan entered the NCAA tournament as a no. 1 seed. Pictured here is Michigan's first round win against Coastal Carolina. Michigan's win could be attributed, in large part, to Jackson's performance on both sides of the court. Offensively, he led the team in scoring for the first time all season, racking in a total of nineteen points, including a perfect 2-for-2 from the line. Yet Coach Fisher emphasized that Jackson's contributions were more than just scoring, explaining that Jackson's defensive performance was crucial to the team's win.

Pictured here is Ray Jackson and the Fab 5 before their game against UCLA in the second round of the NCAA tournament. Jackson scored nineteen points against UCLA, outscored only by Chris Webber and once again proving himself to be one of the keys to Michigan's offensive output. Michigan played a sloppy second half against UCLA but ultimately pulled through with an overtime win to propel them into the Sweet Sixteen.

After a 72–64 win against George Washington and a 77–72 win against Temple (pictured here), Michigan was propelled into its second consecutive Final Four. Jackson was, as usual, a reliable contributor on both sides of the court. He had four rebounds, three assists, and eleven points against George Washington and one rebound, two assists, and ten points against Temple.

Pictured here is Ray Jackson playing defense against Temple. Even though Jackson did not often post particularly high scoring numbers, his intangibles were critical to the team's success. Jackson was known as a hard worker and a strong, reliable defender. This game was played at the Kingdome in Seattle, Washington, in front of an audience of 24,196.

Here is another photo of Jackson's defense against Temple. Michigan's Elite Eight win against Temple happened in large part because of Jackson's tenacious defending.

In the Final Four game against Kentucky, Ray Jackson and Chris Webber were credited for leading the team's defense. Kentucky had beaten its first four NCAA tournament opponents by an average margin of thirty-one points, but Jackson said that Kentucky had not yet faced a defense like Michigan's. He was right. Michigan beat Kentucky 81–78 in overtime, and Jackson ended with eleven points and eight rebounds.

Pictured here is Ray Jackson at a Fab 5 panel in Connecticut. The Final Four game was played at the Louisiana Superdome in New Orleans, for an audience of 64,151. This audience was even bigger than that of their freshman year Final Four game, which was played at the MetroDome in Minneapolis for a crowd of 50,379. Considering Michigan's home arena, Crisler Arena, only seats about 13,000, it is safe to say that the Final Four was an unusually big stage for these five freshmen.

Pictured here is Ray Jackson cutting down the Final Four nets for the second year in a row. Despite his status as the "fifth wheel" in the Fab 5, Jackson memorabilia is still in high demand, sometimes fetching over $100 for a single autographed item on both retail and auction sites. Such income is often a windfall for college athletes, who are, until they leave school, forced to live on a shoestring budget.

After he cut down the nets, Jackson joined an elite group of players to play in multiple national championship games. The award is dubious, however, in two ways as Jackson (and the rest of the Fab 5) are the only teammates to ever forfeit two national championship appearances, and they are, much like the Buffalo Bills in professional football, among a small group to lose two straight championship games.

Pictured here is Jackson playing in the Fab 5's last ever game, the 1993 NCAA championship game, which ended in a heartbreaking loss. Jackson was held to six points, one assist, and zero rebounds. When the players were asked if they were staying at Michigan for another year, Jackson answered, "Me? You know I'm stuck here."

At the end of the Fab 5 era, Jackson was still the least-known member, but he had come to peace with that identity. "I'm the one you might have to think for a second to remember. You go, 'Chris and Jalen, Juwan, Jimmy and, uh ... Ray,'" he told *Sports Illustrated*'s Phil Taylor in April 1993. "But that's cool. I don't need the hype." (*Courtesy of the Bentley Historical Library, University of Michigan*)

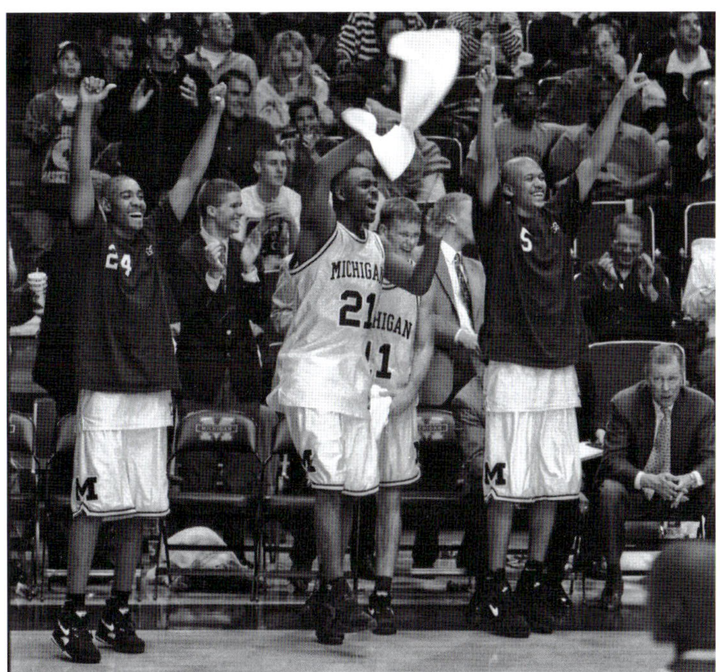

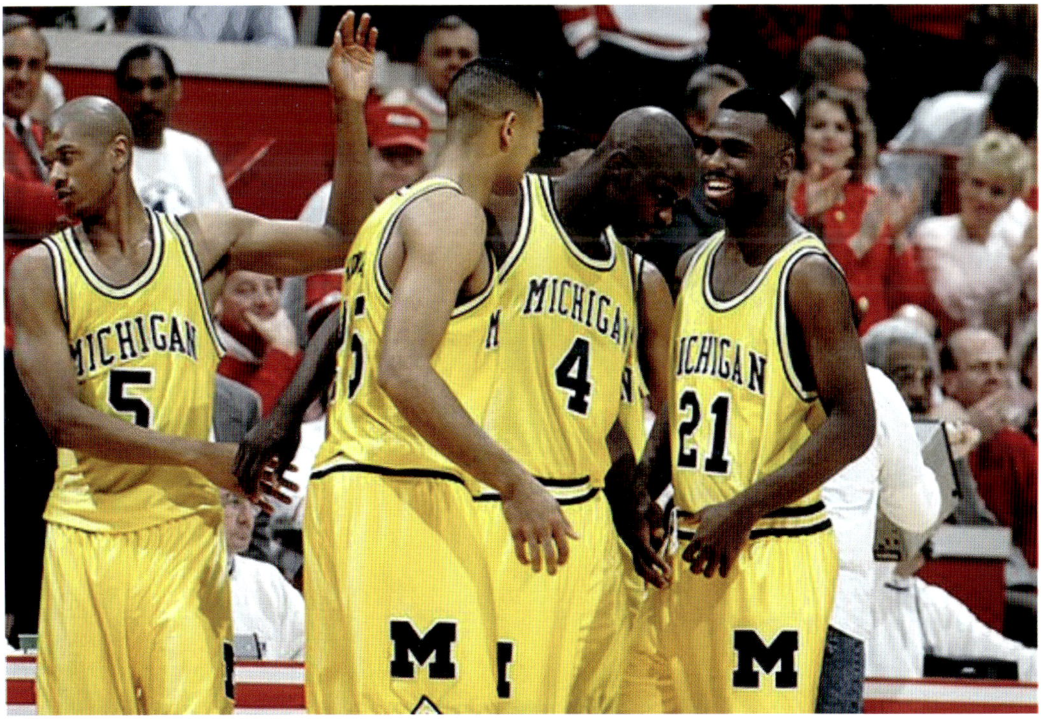

In the 1992–1993 season, Jackson averaged nine points per game, almost doubling his freshman average. That being said, Jackson's most important contributions to the team often came on the defensive end, and therefore are not easily included in box scores and season averages. As Chris Webber left for the NBA, the Wolverines had to find a way to make up for the nineteen points per game that he averaged. Many eyes turned to Jackson, who had established his defensive identity and shown in March that he was capable of scoring as well.

Pictured here is Jackson with teammates Rob Pelinka and Chris Webber. Jackson had a reputation as a team player, which is likely why he was often overlooked. While his teammates consistently produced quotable soundbites and high scoring numbers, Jackson focused on his defensive game and spent his energy supporting the team as a whole.

The beginning of the 1993–1994 season was an adjustment period for Jackson, who, in Webber's absence, had to learn to get comfortable inside the paint. In a preseason game against Croatia, he responded to this adjustment by putting up thirteen points in nineteen minutes. After seeing Jackson's offseason development, fans were hopeful that the team could succeed in Webber's absence.

Pictured here is Jackson defending Purdue forward Glenn Robinson, Jr., whose son Glenn Robinson III would go on to play for Michigan in 2013, which was the next time Michigan would compete for the national title. At this point in the season, Michigan and Purdue led the Big Ten. Jackson finished this game with seven points, one foul, zero assists, and four rebounds.

Michigan entered the 1994 NCAA tournament as no. 3 seed, which is better than many might have predicted given the loss of Chris Webber. Pictured here is Jackson, King, and Rose, during their first-round game against 14-seed Pepperdine, which resulted in a 78–74 overtime win. Public perception of the Wolverines had changed drastically since their freshman year; in the span of two years, Jackson and company had gone from fresh-faced newcomers to bad guys. In the first round, Jackson scored eleven points and had five fouls.

Pictured here is Jackson during Michigan's Sweet Sixteen win against Maryland. Jackson's parents, who came to watch, said that they could feel the pressure just from watching the game. Two days later, Michigan would be eliminated in the Elite Eight after a 68–76 loss to Arkansas. Jackson admitted that it felt "weird" not to play in the Final Four; he and his teammates had not yet experienced staying home and watching another team play on TV.

Jackson finished the 1993–1994 season with an average of 11.4 points, 6.3 rebounds, and 2.6 assists. He and the other remaining Fab 5 members were the only members of the team to average double digits in scoring. Such performance was enough to propel the Steve Fisher-led Wolverines to the Elite Eight.

The accomplishments of Jackson in his career are considerable. Aside from leading the Wolverines in scoring his senior year, Jackson and his Fab 5 cohorts made four straight NCAA Tournament appearances, with two championship appearances, an Elite Eight, and a second-round appearance. Each season ended with both a winning record and a final top twenty-five ranking. Each player would go on to play, in some manner, at the professional level. That is a lot to cheer about, indeed.

Jalen Rose and Juwan Howard both declared for the 1994 NBA draft, leaving Jackson and King as the sole two Fab 5 members to play their senior season. After three seasons observing the leadership of teammates like Webber, Rose, and Howard, Jackson was eager to take on a more vocal leadership role. It took a bit of time for Jackson to adjust to his new role as team leader, but once adjusted, he became the team's biggest asset.

Pictured here is Ray Jackson during a midseason game against St. Johns. Jackson, who scored a career high twenty-seven points in this game, had become Michigan's heart and soul on both sides of the court. Although Michigan ultimately fell 77–82, the game ultimately was not too important because it was a nonconference game in the middle of Big Ten play.

Jackson's senior year, when he was finally freed from the shadows of his teammates, saw him emerge as the team's strongest leader and most valuable player. He led the team in scoring, assists, and free throw percentage, and was second in rebounds. Once the spotlight had finally turned away from Michigan and onto the hot new thing in college basketball, Jackson showed the loyal Michigan fans a glimpse of the superstar he had been in high school. (*Courtesy of the Bentley Historical Library, University of Michigan*)

Jackson is the only member of the Fab 5 who never played in the NBA. He was cut by the New York Knicks in preseason the year after he graduated from Michigan, and the next year, he was cut by the Detroit Pistons in the preseason. In 1995, he was drafted in the Continental Basketball Association by the Grand Rapids Hoops, where he received the 1995–96 CBA Rookie of the Year award. (*Courtesy of the Bentley Historical Library, University of Michigan*)

Above left: Pictured here is Jackson at his *alma mater*, LBJ High School, attending D1 Nation's I-35 challenge in October 2011. Jackson attended as a celebrity judge for the dunk contest. Since retiring from basketball, Jackson has been an engaged member of his communities, both in Texas and Ann Arbor.

Above right: In 2005, Jackson created the Rising Stars Academic and Athletic Program, a nonprofit that provides both educational opportunities and basketball to improve the lives of youth in his hometown of Austin, Texas. Even though the Rising Stars is an AAU program, Jackson chose to emphasize school over sports because of how short-lived most athletic careers are.

Pictured here is Jackson with his son, who participates in the Rising Stars program. Jackson says that his goal with the Rising Stars program was to improve the lives and futures of the kids who participated. Although he supported any of them who wanted to pursue professional basketball, he also encouraged them to obtain an education and reach their goals, whether or not those goals include basketball.

In 2017, Jackson was the keynote speaker at a University of Michigan forum about the stereotypes surrounding black male athletes. He is pictured introducing the audience to his former teammate Jimmy King, who also spoke in the forum. In the forum, Jackson recalled the athletic pressure he felt during his time at Michigan, and how that pressure often compromised his academics.

More than twenty-five years after the Fab 5 era, Jackson continues to support Michigan basketball. Pictured here is Jackson repping the maize and blue at the Frank Erwin Center in Austin, Texas, where the Wolverines traveled to beat the Longhorns 59–52. Even though Jackson has lived in Austin for most of his life, he was not afraid to wear his gear in a sea of burnt orange.

Pictured here is Jackson at his alma mater, Lyndon B. Johnson High School. This photo is from a 2018 interview before the Michigan Wolverines competed once again for the NCAA title. In the interview, Jackson shared that he would be rooting for Michigan to win the championship, which would be played in his home state of Texas.

Even though Jackson has a fulfilling career and life that exist completely separate from his Fab 5 legacy, he remains loyal to the maize and blue. It is not uncommon to see Jackson with his Fab 5 teammates, at introspective events, Michigan games, or interviews on platforms such as ESPN and TNT. Despite opinions to the contrary, Jackson is, in no way, shape or form, a "fifth wheel". Rather, Jackson, just as with his classmates, is one of the equal parts of the Fab 5, basketball's most iconic recruiting class.

6
THE
FAB 5
HOWARD, JACKSON, KING, ROSE, AND WEBBER

OTHER NAMES: 5 Times (Stylized 5X's)

INSTITUTION: The University of Michigan

HEAD COACH: Steve Fisher

SEASONS: 1991–1995

CONFERENCE: The Big Ten

LOCATION: Ann Arbor, Michigan

ARENA: Crisler Arena

TEAMMATES: Chip Armer, Eric Riley, Michael Talley, James Voskuil, Rob Pelinka, Freddie Hunter, Rich McIver, Sam Mitchell, Kirk Taylor, Jason Bossard, Chris Seter, Leon Derricks, Dugan Fife, Sean Dobbins, Ricky Guzman, Tariq Abdul-Wahad, Bobby Crawford, Makhtar N'Diaye, Chris Fields, Emerson Moore, Seth Smith, Maurice Taylor, Maceo Baston, Willie Mitchell, Jerod Ward, Travis Conlan, Neal Morton, and Alex Lengemann.

FUTURE NBA PLAYERS: Chris Webber, Jalen Rose, Juwan Howard, Jimmy King, Eric Riley, Makhtar N'Diaye, Maurice Taylor, and Maceo Baston.

COACH STEVE FISHER

ACCOMPLISHMENTS: NCAA Division I Tournament Champion (1989); NCAA Regional—Final Four (1989, 1992, 1993); NIT (1997); Mountain West Conference Tournament (2002, 2006, 2010, 2011); MWC regular season (2006, 2011, 2012, 2014–2016); Naismith College Coach of the Year (2011); NABC Coach of the Year (2011); Wooden Legends of Coaching Award (2015); MWC Coach of the Year (2011, 2012, 2014, 2016); Adolph Rupp Cup (2011).

BY THE SEASON

SEASON	WINS	LOSSES	CONFERENCE W-L	RESULT
1991–1992	25	9	11–7	NCAA Runner-Up
1992–1993	31	5	15–3	NCAA Runner-Up
1993–1994	24	8	13–5	NCAA Elite Eight
1994–1995	17	14	11–7	NCAA Round of 64

Chip Armer is one of the lesser-known players from the Fab 5 era. He transferred to Michigan as a part of the Fab 5 recruiting class. Previously, he had played a year at West Point and a year with Santa Fe Community College. Due to the amazing amount of talent that arrived when he did, Armer would only see action in eight Wolverine games during his tenure. In those eight games, he tallied twelve minutes, four points, one block, a turnover, and two fouls. Today, Armer is the head basketball coach at Manatee High School in Florida. (*Courtesy of the Bentley Historical Library, University of Michigan*)

Dugan Fife arrived a year after the Fab 5 exploded on the scene. A 6-foot 3-inch shooting guard, Fife played his entire four-year career with at least one member of the Fab 5. Fife averaged 4.1 points, two rebounds, and 1.8 assists in his career. He did so on 36.3 percent career shooting. After his career at Michigan, which included appearances in the Final Four, the Sweet Sixteen, and the second round of the NCAA tournament, Fife would later work as a national sales manager for Hines Securities. (*Courtesy of the Bentley Historical Library, University of Michigan*)

Eric Riley was the "sixth man" when it came to the Fab 5 years. An injured redshirt freshman when Michigan won the 1989 NCAA title, Riley would go from All Big 10 to super reserve, augmenting the youthful power of the Fab 5 with a steady hand on the boards and on defense. He averaged, in 126 career games, 6.2 points, 5.2 rebounds, and half an assist. Drafted by the Dallas Mavericks with the thirty-third pick in the second round of the 1993 NBA Draft, he would be traded to the Houston Rockets, where he would win an NBA championship in 1994, before playing with the Clippers, Timberwolves, Mavericks, Celtics, and several overseas franchises. (*Courtesy of the Bentley Historical Library, University of Michigan*)

Another player supplanted once the Fab 5 hit campus, James Voskuil still played a key role in the Wolverine's plans. Voskuil would play ninety-five games for the Wolverines, with twenty-eight starts. In an average of 14.7 minutes per game, Voskuil would average 3.9 points, two rebounds, and less than an assist, a steal, and a block per game. Nonetheless, Voskuil was accurate from behind the arc, finishing his career above 40 percent from a three-point land. After leaving Michigan, he would spend preseason time in the NBA with Detroit and Seattle before playing in Finland, and France, where he played for seven different clubs. (*Courtesy of the Bentley Historical Library, University of Michigan*)

Although he would only play with two members of the Fab 5, Jerod Ward was a blue-chip recruit in his own right. The 1994 high school player of the year, Ward would sign with Michigan, where he would help lead the Wolverines to the 1997 NIT championship. In ninety-nine games at Michigan, Ward average 9.4 points, 4.5 rebounds, and less than one assist, steal, and block per game. Undrafted by the NBA, Ward would spend time with teams in the Continental Basketball Association, the International Basketball League, the American Basketball Association, and in the Philippines, Spain, France, South Korea, Italy, Lebanon, Japan, and Venezuela. (*Courtesy of the Bentley Historical Library, University of Michigan*)

Kirk Taylor was a key player in Michigan's 1988–1989 national championship season and played a key reserve role in the 1991–1992 national runner-up season alongside the Fab 5. In seventy-eight career games with Michigan, with sixteen starts, Taylor averaged 5.4 points, 2.4 rebounds, 1.6 assists, and less than one steal and one block per game. Taylor's father was also a Detroit sports legend before playing football at Howard University. His brother, Keith, played football at the University of Cincinnati. (*Courtesy of the Bentley Historical Library, University of Michigan*)

Once a top-ten candidate for Michigan's Mr. Basketball, Leon Derricks hit Ann Arbor a year after the Fab 5 came to play for Coach Fisher. Given the deep, talented roster that was in place, Derricks saw sparse playing time, averaging, in forty-four games, 1.8 points, 1.9 rebounds, and less than one assist, steal, and block per game. He transferred to Detroit Mercy and, after sitting out a season, played two more, averaging 9.9 points, 6.2 rebounds, and 1.2 assists per game. He later played professionally in South Korea and Poland. (*Courtesy of the Bentley Historical Library, University of Michigan*)

Maceo Baston would spend the first two years of his college career playing with Fab 5ers Jimmy King and Ray Jackson. In four years at Michigan, Baston would average 10.6 points, 7.4 rebounds, 1.2 assists, 1.1 blocks, and less than one steal per game. Drafted in the second round of the 1998 NBA draft by the Chicago Bulls, Baston would play 105 career NBA games for the Pacers and Raptors before playing professionally in the Continental Basketball Association and in Italy, Spain, Israel, and Ukraine, where he would win two Euroleague and three Israeli League championships. (*Courtesy of the Bentley Historical Library, University of Michigan*)

Maurice Taylor came to Michigan at the tail end of the Fab 5 era and spent two seasons playing with Jimmy King and Ray Jackson. In three years and ninety-eight games at Michigan, Taylor averaged 12.9 points, 6.1 rebounds, 1.2 assists, and less than one steal and one block per game. His success led to him being the fourteenth overall pick by the Los Angeles Clippers in the 1997 NBA draft. He would play in the NBA for the Clippers, Rockets, Knicks, and Kings, making the all-rookie second team in 1998. He would later play professionally in Spain and China. (*Courtesy of the Bentley Historical Library, University of Michigan*)

Michael Talley was the 1989 Mr. Basketball for the state of Michigan before matriculating at the University of Michigan, to play basketball under coach Steve Fisher. His arrival would predate the Fab 5 by one year. In three seasons and eighty-seven games, Talley would average 5.8 points, 1.5 rebounds, 2.1 assists, and less than one steal and one block per game. He would start forty-three of those games. He played his high school basketball at Detroit Cooley High School and would be a part of two NCAA runner-up teams in his time at Michigan. (*Courtesy of the Bentley Historical Library, University of Michigan*)

Shown here is Neal Morton, who played two seasons with members of the Fab 5. In thirty-three games, Morton averaged less than a point and a rebound and less than a half of an assist, steal, and block per game. Morton's work off the court is his true calling card, as he went on to become a vice president at Barton Marlow Company, a business focused on construction. *Building Construction and Design* named him one of their "40 under 40" for 2011. He was also known for the vast amount of charity work he did with the University of Michigan's Mott Children's Hospital. (*Courtesy of the Bentley Historical Library, University of Michigan*)

Although three members of the Fab 5 may make it into the Naismith Hall of Fame for their exploits around the game, it could be argued that Rob Pelinka has had a bigger impact on the sport than any of them. A four-year star at Michigan, Pelinka would go on to graduate from law school in 1996. Upon graduation, he would become the agent for Kobe Bryant, perhaps one of the greatest players in NBA history. His success as an agent would lead to his being name the general manager of the Los Angeles Lakers, where he played a key role in bringing LeBron James to L.A. (*Courtesy of the Bentley Historical Library, University of Michigan*)

Travis Conlan played with four of the five members of the Fab 5 during his time as a Wolverine. He was a member of the 1997 NIT and the 1998 Big 10 Championship teams. He would play overseas for eleven years, playing in the ABA, the CBA, and in England, Greece, Germany, Poland, and Belgium. He would serve as Michigan's director of basketball operations from 2010 to 2013, before resigning to pursue a career in coaching. He remains in fifth place in both assists and steals among Michigan players. (*Courtesy of the Bentley Historical Library, University of Michigan*)

Willie Dion Mitchell III was a part of Michigan's most heralded recruiting class since the Fab 5, and he played one season with both Ray Jackson and Jimmy King at Michigan. He was Michigan's Mr. Basketball in 1994. In his two years at Michigan, he averaged 5.4 points, 2.8 rebounds, and less than an assist, a steal, and a block per game. He would play his final two years at Alabama-Birmingham before playing professionally in the ABA, the CBA, the IBA, and in China, Finland, and Poland. (*Courtesy of the Bentley Historical Library, University of Michigan*)

This is a team photo of the 1991–1992 University of Michigan basketball team. *From left to right, front row*: Jalen Rose, Kirk Taylor, Jason Bossard, Michael Talley, coach Steve Fisher, Freddie Hunter, Rob Pelinka, Ray Jackson, and Jimmy King. *Back row*: Troy Amaris, Brian Dutcher, Chris Seter, James Voskuil, Chris Webber, Chip Armer, Eric Riley, Juwan Howard, Rich McIver, Sam Mitchell, Jay Smith, and Perry Watson. (*Courtesy of the Bentley Historical Library, University of Michigan*)

This photo was taken of the Michigan Wolverines Basketball team in 1992 and includes each member of the Fab 5. *From left to right, back row*: (unknown), assistant coach Brian Dutcher, Chris Seter, James Voskuil, Harry (Chip) Armer, Eric Riley, Juwan Howard, Rich McIver, Samuel Mitchell, assistant coach Jay Smith, and assistant coach Perry Watson. *Front row*: Jalen Rose, Kirk Taylor, Jason Bossard, Michal Talley, Frederick Hunter, Rob Pelinka, Ray Jackson, and Jimmy King. (*Courtesy of the Bentley Historical Library, University of Michigan*)

This photo shows the 1992–1993 Michigan Wolverines basketball team, which included all five members of the Fab 5. *Back row*: Ray Jackson, Jalen Rose, Jimmy King, Chris Webber, Eric Riley, Juwan Howard, Leon Derricks, and James Voskuil. *Front row*: Rick Guzman, Dugan Fife, Jimmy King, Michael Talley, Rob Pelinka, Jason Bossard, and Sean Dobbins. (*Courtesy of the Bentley Historical Library, University of Michigan*)

This is a photo, taken outdoors, of the 1992–1993 national runner-up Michigan Wolverines basketball team, which included all five members of the Fab 5, including Wooden Player of the Year Chris Webber. *From left to right, back row*: (unknown), Jalen Rose, Chris Webber, Eric Riley, Juwan Howard, Leon Derricks, James Voskuil, and coach Steve Fisher. *Front row*: Sean Dobbins, Rob Pelinka, Ray Jackson, Michael Talley, Jason Bossard, Jimmy King, and Dugan Fife. (*Courtesy of the Bentley Historical Library, University of Michigan*)

This photo shows the 1993–1994 Michigan Wolverines basketball team, with the players standing in a semicircle around half court. Every member of the Fab 5 except for Chris Webber, who had left for the NBA, is in this photo. *From left to right*: Bobby Crawford, Dugan Fife, Jimmy King, Jalen Rose, Juwan Howard, Leon Derricks, Ray Jackson, Olivier Saint-Jean, Chris Fields, and Jason Bossard. (*Courtesy of the Bentley Historical Library, University of Michigan*)

Shown in this photo are the 1993–1994 Michigan Wolverines, who, thanks to the play of Fab 5 members Jalen Rose, Ray Jackson, Juwan Howard, and Jimmy King, made it to the NCAA Tournament Elite Eight. *From left to right, back row*: assistant coach Brian Dutcher, assistant coach Jay Smith, Chris Fields, Leon Derricks, Juwan Howard, Olivier Saint-Jean, Jimmy King, coach Steve Fisher, and assistant coach Scott Perry. *Front row*: equipment manager Bob Bland, Jalen Rose, Bobby Crawford, Jason Bossard, Dugan Fife, Ray Jackson, and trainer David Ralston. (*Courtesy of the Bentley Historical Library, University of Michigan*)

Shown in this photo is the 1994–1995 Michigan Wolverines basketball team, which included Fab 5 members Jimmy King and Ray Jackson. *From left to right, back row*: academic advisor Bob Clifford, trainer David Ralston, assistant coach Jay Smith, assistant coach Brian Dutcher, assistant coach Scott Perry, strength trainer Jim Plocki, and equipment manager Bob Bland. *Middle row*: Neal Morton, Bobby Crawford, Dugan Fife, Willie Mitchell, Olivier Saint-Jean, Travis Conlan, and Adam Jones. *Front row*: Maceo Baston, Makhtar Ndiaye, Ray Jackson, Jimmy King, Jerod Ward, and Maurice Taylor. (*Courtesy of the Bentley Historical Library, University of Michigan*)

Shown here with a loose, baggy pair of Michigan Wolverine shorts, are the Nike Air Max 5 basketball shoes. By the time the 1993 NCAA Tournament rolled around, the entirety of the Fab 5 would be outfitted with a pair of these shoes. Matching the pulled-up black socks that the quintet wore, Nike engineered these shoes for both performance and comfort, with an air bubble in the heel for extra padding and thick, yet lightweight insulation for cushion and comfort, these shoes would also be worn by the likes of Charles Barkley, then a member of the Phoenix Suns. Nike would release a commemorative pair in 2006, named after the Fab 5.

Shown in this photograph is coach Steve Fisher, the recruiting genius behind the Fab 5. After taking over on the eve of the 1989 NCAA tournament, Fisher did the impossible and led the Wolverines to the 1989 NCAA championship. He would lead the Wolverines to the 1992 and 1993 national championship games as well. His accolades at Michigan also include an Elite Eight, three other tournament appearances, and two NIT appearances, including a win in 1997. After his time at Michigan, he would coach at San Diego State, leading the Aztecs to eight NCAA tournament appearances and five NIT appearances. He retired in 2017. (*Courtesy of the Bentley Historical Library, University of Michigan*)

Shown here with Fab 5 member Jalen Rose is Perry Watson, who was Rose's high school head coach before taking an assistant coaching job at Michigan when Rose committed. After spending two years at Michigan, Watson took the head coaching job at the University of Detroit-Mercy, a post that he held until 2008. Watson twice led the Titans to the Horizon League regular-season title, and twice to the Horizon League tournament. He led Detroit to their first NCAA Tournament wins since 1977. Watson would retire in 2008 due to health concerns. (*Courtesy of the Bentley Historical Library, University of Michigan*)

Shown in this picture, with coach Steve Fisher, are Jalen Rose, Juwan Howard, Ray Jackson, and Jimmy King, the remnants of the Fab 5 after Chris Webber's departure for the NBA. In three seasons together, this trio would appear in two NCAA Championship games and one Elite Eight. The four averaged 52.14 points per game, making up the majority of the team's scoring during the era. They would compile an 80–22 record, including a mark of 39–15 in the Big 10. (*Courtesy of the Bentley Historical Library, University of Michigan*)

The players that make up the Fab 5 each came from distinct backgrounds. Chris Webber led the prestigious, private Detroit Country Day School to three state championships. Jalen Rose attended the now closed, inner-city Detroit Southwestern High School. Juwan Howard was an honors student at the Chicago Vocational Career Academy. Jimmy King played his high school basketball at Plano East High School in Plano, Texas, and Ray Jackson played at Lyndon B. Johnson High School in Austin, Texas, where he later coached. (*Courtesy of the Bentley Historical Library, University of Michigan*)

Each of the Fab 5 also had professional basketball experience. Chris Webber would be taken no. 1 overall by the Orlando Magic, and would play for the Warriors, Bullets, Wizards, Kings, 76ers, and Piston. Jalen Rose was selected by the Denver Nuggets and would play for the Pacers, Bulls, Raptors, Knicks, and Suns. Juwan Howard was drafted by the Bullets and would also play for the Wizards, Mavericks, Nuggets, Magic, Rockets, Bobcats, Trail Blazers, and Heat. Jimmy King was drafted by the Raptors and would play for the Mavericks, Nuggets, Pacers, in the CBA the IBL, and in Venezuela and Poland. Ray Jackson Played in the CBA for the Grand Rapids Hoops. (*Courtesy of the Bentley Historical Library, University of Michigan*)

Each member of the Fab 5 would go on to various post-basketball success as well. Ray Jackson coached at his former high school before opening a moving company and a basketball nonprofit called Ray Jackson's Rising Stars. Jimmy King runs a community foundation for Detroit youth, owns a solar panel company, and coached high school basketball. Juwan Howard is currently an assistant coach with the Miami Heat. Jalen Rose is a commentator for ESPN and founded the Jalen Rose Leadership Academy in Detroit. Chris Webber is a commentator for TNT and owns an extensive collection of African American artifacts. (*Courtesy of the Bentley Historical Library, University of Michigan*)

Shown here are Juwan Howard, Jalen Rose, and Chris Webber, who would go on to have the most professional success of the Fab 5 recruiting class. Howard would make the All-Star team in 1996, in addition to being named third team all-NBA. He would also win two championships with the Miami Heat. Jalen Rose would be named "Most Improved Player" in 2000 and was a member of the NBA's all-rookie second team in 1995. Webber would play in five all-star games, be named All-NBA first team once, second team three times, and third team once. He was named "Rookie of the Year" in 1994 and led the NBA in rebounds in 1999.

Statistically, the three would also put up impressive professional stat lines. For his career, Webber would average 20.7 points, 9.8 rebounds, 4.2 assists, 1.4 steals, and 1.4 blocks per game, while averaging 37.1 minutes per game. Jalen Rose would average 14.3 points, 3.5 rebounds, 3.8 assists, 0.8 steals, and 0.3 blocks per game, while averaging a robust 30.3 minutes per game. Juwan Howard would average 13.4 points, 6.1 rebounds, 2.2 assists, 0.7 steals, and 0.3 blocks per game while averaging 30.3 minutes per game.

Shown here are members of the Fab 5 wearing blue uniforms for a road game. The use of blue by the University dates back all the way to before the rise of collegiate sports, when, in 1867, members of the literary department met on February 12. In this meeting, the panel decided that the blue that made up the Michigan uniform would be "azure-blue". Without a definition of what "azure-blue" was supposed to be, many color variations showed up. This was cause for another meeting in 1912, when the actual tone of blue that Michigan would use was decided on. The committee called for a darker blue, as opposed to the sky blue that had become the norm.

This photo shows the Fab 5 huddled up while wearing their "maize" colored uniforms, which stand today as the basketball team's "alternate" home uniforms. Maize became the school's primary color when, on February 12, 1867, members of the literature department met to decide what the school's colors would be. "Maize" was chosen to be the school's flagship color. In 1912, maize was defined as "the color of corn," while it was stressed that lemon yellow should be avoided at all costs. The 1912 color swatches reside in the Bentley Historical Library massive archive.

Shown here sitting on chairs, the Fab 5 sport their white uniforms, which, by NCAA standards, are always wore by the home team. In addition to standing in contrast to the quintuplets pulled-up black socks, these uniforms proved to be a sign of great success for the group. In the two years that all five were in Ann Arbor, they compiled a 25–5 record at Crisler Arena. Four of those five losses would come against teams ranked thirteenth or higher, and four of those five games would be decided by five points or less.

Shown here are Fab 5 members Chris Webber, Jalen Rose, and Juwan Howard, in a break in the action during their 1993 showdown with fierce intrastate rival Michigan State. The teams have played an incredible 190 times since their first meeting on January 9, 1909, which was won by Michigan Agricultural (now Michigan State) by a tally of 24–16. Michigan holds at 93–84 all time advantage, which includes this game, where the seventh-ranked Wolverines beat the twenty-fifth-ranked Spartans by a score of 73–69. (*Courtesy of the Bentley Historical Library, University of Michigan*)

After Webber declared for the NBA Draft, four members of the Fab 5 remained. The games had to go on, and so they did. This photo shows Jalen Rose huddled with Fab 5'ers Juwan Howard, Jimmy King, and Ray Jackson, along with Dugan Fife, during a home game with intrastate rival Central Michigan on Monday, December 20, 1993. The game was a blowout, with the seventh-ranked Wolverines dominating the unranked Chippewas by a tally of 86–44. The win moved the Wolverines record to 6–1, with their sole loss on the season coming to fourth-ranked Duke only nine days prior. (*Courtesy of the Bentley Historical Library, University of Michigan*)

This photo shows Fab 5 members Jalen Rose and Juwan Howard playing tough defense against Wisconsin during the Wolverines home game against the Badgers on Saturday, January 29, 1994. The fifteenth-ranked Wolverines managed to come out on top of the sixteenth-ranked Badgers by a final tally of 79–75. The win would move the Wolverines to a 13–4 record on the season and was the second of a nine-game winning streak that would be halted by the same Wisconsin team on March 2, this time in Madison. (*Courtesy of the Bentley Historical Library, University of Michigan*)

This photo shows the Fab 5 in a jovial mood with coach Steve Fisher before the 1992–1993 season. As far as recruiting goes, the class one of the most historic in history, with four of the five being ranked in the top ten of all high school prospects (Webber no. 1; Howard no. 3; Rose no. 5, and King no. 9) and all five (with the addition of eighty-fourth-ranked Ray Jackson) being within the Top 100. Webber, Rose, Jackson, and King would all play in the 1991 McDonald's All-Star game, where Webber would be named MVP. The five would see the court together for the first time on December 7, 1991, against Eastern Michigan. (*Courtesy of the Bentley Historical Library, University of Michigan*)

Although shown here making a hand gesture that paid homage to their own name for themselves (Five Times), the place in Michigan lore that the Fab 5 holds cannot be disputed. In fact, despite the great success that Michigan sports had at the time (which included the 1989 NCAA tournament, back-to-back Frozen Fours for the Michigan hockey team, and both Desmond Howard's Heisman Trophy and five straight Big Ten titles in football, capped off by an unbeaten season in 1992), on campus, the Fab 5 were king, far outselling any other team in terms of merchandise. (*Courtesy of the Bentley Historical Library, University of Michigan*)

Shown standing under a ladder at Crisler Arena, the members of the Fab 5 can only be anticipating the success they would have. Twice, they were the national runner-up in the NCAA tournament, in addition to an Elite Eight and a fourth berth in the tournament. They would go on to successful pro careers in the NBA, the CBA, and abroad, leading to championships, personal honors, and success on and off the basketball court. While some would argue that the failure of the group to win a NCAA championship is a ding against their record, there can be no question that the Fab 5 is one of the most successful recruiting classes of all time.

Their impact on the world cannot be understated. Chris Webber has gathered an extensive collection of African-American artifacts on slavery, which have been on display at the Sacramento Public Library, at Weber State University, at the Crocker Art Museum, and at the Charles H. Wright Museum of African American History in Detroit. Rose has started the Jalen Rose Leadership Academy in Detroit for at-risk youth. Juwan Howard runs the Juwan Howard Foundation in DC for at-risk youth and visited countless patients at the University of Michigan hospital while a player. Ray Jackson runs Ray Jackson's Rising Stars in Texas, to help youth on and off the court. Jimmy King is the program director of H.Y.P.E. Athletics Community, a nonprofit organization which provides academic, athletic, and citizenship mentoring for youth in the Detroit area. (*Courtesy of the Bentley Historical Library, University of Michigan*)